The Modern Paradigm of Liberty

An Uncommon Sense Viewpoint on Contemporary American Issues

By

Sean McPhillips

This limited edition of The Modern Paradigm of Liberty was printed as an **advance market review copy** for promotional purposes and is not for resale. As such, there are various typographical errors due to this being printed before final edit. Additionally, some content supplements have also been added for further clarity. Retail market copies of this book have all content changes and typographical errors integrated into the final edit. Please accept this imperfect copy with both my apologies and compliments. I hope you enjoy reading it as much as I had writing it. Thank you.

© 2003 by Sean McPhillips. All rights reserved.

No part of this book may be reproduced, stored in a retrieval system, or transmitted by any means, electronic, mechanical, photocopying, recording, or otherwise, without written permission from the author.

ISBN: 1-4140-2690-0 (e-book)
ISBN: 1-4140-2689-7 (Paperback)
ISBN: 1-4140-2688-9 (Dust Jacket)

Library of Congress Control Number: 2003098177

This book is printed on acid free paper.

Printed in the United States of America
Bloomington, IN

1stBooks - rev. 11/14/03

Table of Contents

Forward v
The Republican Federation 1
The Mission of the United States Constitution 5
The Confederate Battle Flag 11
Morals, Ethics and Government 15
World Government 21
Contingency Government for Disaster Recovery 33
Volunteer Marshal Corps 39
Capital Punishment 45
Accountability of Parole Boards 49
Circumventing Due Process 53
Case Law Review 59
The Basic Flaws of Criminal Adjudication 63
Atheism versus Socialism 69
Marriage versus Civil Unions 73
Teamwork 79
President Andrew Johnson 83
So-Called Liberalism 87
Celebrity 91
Discrimination 95
What Does Pro-Choice Really Mean? 99
Public Breast Feeding 105
The Healthcare Customer 107

Suing Health Insurance Providers	111
Priests and Pedophilia	115
Meagan's Law	119
Eroding Freedoms	123
Airport Security and the Fourth Amendment	131
Desecration of the American Flag	137
The Pledge of Allegiance	141
Sexual Freedom	149
Slavery Reparations	153
The Arrogance of Man	159
The Electoral College	165
Voter Nullification	171
Consumption Taxation	175
The Stock Market	183
The Economics of School Vouchers	189
Taxation without Representation	193
The Politics of Heaven	197
The Ten Commandments	205
School Prayer	213
Science of the Soul	217
Stigmata, Shroud and Fatima	223
In God We Trust	231
The Separation of Church and State	235
Summary	241
Favorite Quotes of the Author	243

Forward

The pages that follow represent subjective opinions on various subjects in contemporary American society. In your reading, you may construe some positions as conservative while others liberal. While the discussions of this author will be obviously inconsistent with the traditional blanket platforms of both positions, all positions taken in this book are based on the following universal principle of liberty and freedom.

*The inalienable right of **everyone** in a free society is that they are all entitled to life, liberty and the pursuit of happiness. And, in the exercise of the former, no one individual's or group of individuals' rights shall infringe on the rights of anyone else.*

This is the basic principle that governs any society that claims to be **free**. Furthermore, the application of this principle domestically has had a dynamic history since the Declaration of Independence. Most notable is slavery.

While the founding fathers conceived this concept of ideal liberty, they were only able to practice what was considered to be pragmatic liberty for their period. However, their wisdom embodied in the United States Constitution has allowed the document and our society to grow and mature as liberty and freedom in the United States expands.

Through the centuries, while some liberties have broadened and other narrowed, we as Americans still practice the practical application of liberty and freedom. This book challenges the reader to consider the potential of the United States as we continue to grow and aspire towards a truly free society for *all* Americans. Furthermore, it challenges many actions of government and/or the majority intended to restrict or limit any individual liberties of any Americans.

In the discussions that follow, the average reader would likely agree with some positions, while disagree with others. None of these discussions are specifically designed to change the reader's position on issues, but rather to invoke the reader to think in a different light on many issues that have otherwise been beaten to death with the same old arguments.

The unique perspectives on current issues in American society suggested in the pages that follow apparently escapes the common sense of those subject matter experts discussing these issues publicly. Collectively, they comprise what this author believes to be the modern paradigm of liberty and the contemporary fruition of the founders' vision. The hope is that you, the reader, will come away with a new perspective on many issues and, perhaps, think a little more objectively instead of what is repeatedly spoken by others.

The United States is the oldest functioning example of a government of the people, by the people and for the people. This book represents this author's unilateral commitment to a free society, conceived by the founding fathers, and a continuous challenge for Americans to aspire towards the perfect model of freedom and liberty for all.

Author's Supplement:

In the ongoing struggle for liberty in American history, the battle lines have always been drawn between two basic groups. One side fights for liberty; to either maintain an established freedom or broaden liberty in ways never before. The other side fights against liberty; to either curb an established freedom or rationalize the perpetuation of an institutionalized liberty infringement. Historically and appropriately in American history, those fighting for liberty are consistently victorious over those fighting against liberty.

Examples of this thesis include the abolishment of slavery, women's suffrage, and the civil rights movement. Contemporary American society is no exception.

In general, the modern paradigm of liberty is the independent and free-thinking thought process of every contemporary American. More specifically, this book illustrates **my** subjective paradigm, but guides you through my reasoning processes, which will either reinforce your opinions if you agree with me, or require you to reconcile my points should you disagree with me.

Additionally, some essays may even seem loosely tied to liberty in the traditional sense, but they relate to the overall theme because they illustrate the independent, free-thought process necessary for a contemporary American citizen to effectively form their own opinions, which in turn impacts society and liberty as a whole.

My hope here is that if these discussions can get you to think more objectively about your belief system in a contemporary light, then you might be more open to an evolving free society.

The Republican Federation

This discussion is not a stance or a position on any issue, but merely a statement of fact. The purpose of this discussion is to lay a principle foundation for many of the future arguments presented in later readings.

First, let us examine and better understand what the concept of the "United States" really means. In many countries (for example, Portugal, Israel, and Liberia), when referring to "the state government", such reference is actually to the National Government. But in the United States, this is obviously not the case. The origins of this distinction dates back to the very foundation of the nation.

Though the nation was founded in 1776 and the U.S. Constitution was first introduced in 1787, the U.S. Constitution did not officially take effect until 1789. So, what did we do for 13 years? We had the Articles of Confederation. This document loosely constructed the "national" governing body and originally framed the United States as a confederacy. Furthermore, within a confederacy, there is not only a great deal of autonomy among the member states, but also the discretion to reject federal law.

However, the confederacy was too weak of a model that it failed to establish sufficient cohesion of the states, which jeopardized the long-term success as a unified government. Hence, this lead to the Constitutional Convention, which produced the United States Constitution. To date, the U.S. Constitution remains as the oldest, and most mature active model of freedom and democracy in the world.

Different from the Articles of Confederation, the U.S. Constitution structured this nation as a federation, by which all member states subscribe to and recognize such federal authority as supreme compared to the government of each state. However, the mission of the national government was not to micromanage the states, as the states still retain a great deal of autonomy, which is clearly asserted by the 10th Amendment.

But the founders quickly recognized a basic flaw with the democracy model, and that was the tyranny of the majority. In an absolute democracy, the majority can assert their collective will on minorities or individuals and infringe on their liberties. The simplest example of a pure democracy is five wolves and a sheep voting on dinner. Recognizing this to be a threat to a free society, the founders gave us the Bill of Rights and asserted this democracy as a republic.

Interestingly, the United States is also the most experienced model of unified governments in the world. While other unifications have failed or under performed in the past (League of Nations and United Nations), the United States continues to build its strength by celebrating its diversity and cherishing its liberties. The failure of these other so-called international models is largely due to the concessions of freedoms and liberties that are made in order to subscribe to their socialist philosophies. This is explored in more detail in later discussions.

So, think of it this way, the United States is, in reality, a federation of nation-states and not simply a country. Throughout the years, this approach has allowed the United States to develop a tight cohesion among member states and have melted our image into a single identity. This is not a detriment as it illustrates that a government designed as a federation of nation-states dedicated to continuously aspire towards pure individual freedom and liberty, as well as the ability to grow and mature with time, will ultimately lead to the best society for mankind.

The Mission of the United States Constitution

Both the political Right and Left have used the U.S. Constitution as the basis for legal arguments in our society and both sides tend to claim that the U.S. Constitution supports their argument and not the others. But how can that be? The U.S. Constitution and its subsequent amendments are very clear, concise and to the point. There should be no room for debate or ambiguity, but somehow there is. Perhaps, this is due to the misunderstanding of what the mission of the U.S. Constitution really is.

First and foremost, the mission of the U.S. Constitution is to define the **structure** of the American government. Articles I, II, and III specifically lay the foundation for the federal architecture of the national government. To put it simply, it defines the blueprint by which the government is formed and maintained. Each of these three articles is dedicated to one of the three branches of government and designed to establish the separation of powers. Without this, one branch could assume more control over the other and violate such separation.

This was the basis of the impeachment trial of Andrew Johnson as Congress passed a law to restrict Presidential discretion on cabinet assignments. President Johnson overtly broke that law with the argument that such law violated the separation principle, and was ultimately vindicated because of the unconstitutionality of the law.

Second, the mission of the U.S. Constitution is to define the **powers** of government. The specifically enumerated powers of the federal government are throughout the body of the Articles, but most attention is paid to Article I, Section 8, which enumerates the powers of Congress. The most significant element of this section is the *"necessary and proper clause"*, which empowers Congress to make laws, which shall be necessary and proper for carrying into execution any of its enumerated powers. This clause is the most likely culprit for the creation of most administrative agencies.

Most administrative agencies are NOT specifically enumerated as powers of government but are deemed necessary and proper for the execution of effective governance. For example, Congress has the specifically enumerated power to collect taxes, but not to establish the IRS. However, the IRS is deemed necessary and proper to carry out the execution for the collection of income taxes, thus making the IRS Constitutionally sound.

Last, but not least, the mission of the U.S. Constitution is to **define the rights** of individual citizens. A free society can only be a free society if freedom applies to everyone. The founders initially framed this federation as a democracy, but quickly realized that such paradigm has a critical flaw, which is the tyranny of the majority and can result in the infringement of liberties on individuals. This flaw was corrected with the Bill of Rights and asserted our democracy as a republic.

Throughout the Bill of Rights, there are numerous references to the people, all of which are the rights that are entitled to any citizen living in a free society. This is by no means a complete list, but a substantially sound list to build from. Wherever possible, individual liberties should be broadly construed as long as said liberties do not infringe on the liberties of others when exercised. The Bill of Rights concludes with the 10th Amendment, which clearly states that any powers not specifically enumerated to the federal government default to the several states and/or people.

This protects the individual sovereignty of the states, allows for great latitude of discretion at the state level, and empowers the people to have a more intimate relationship with their government for issues that relate to their local region. Similarly, states apply this same concept to their lower levels of government. Therefore, this model by design does not require the federal government to micro govern the people.

However, both the Right and the Left often argue that if the U.S. Constitution omits something that somehow the opposite therefore applies. This is often used in the context of government restrictions. The U.S. Constitution was never intended to restrict the powers of government, i.e. what government and/or the people "can't" do. If that were the case, the U.S. Constitution would fill a library instead of four pages. The only exception is the 18th Amendment, which prohibited alcohol. Appropriately, this is the only amendment that was repealed by another Constitutional amendment, further asserting the true mission of the Constitution.

Inversely, by referring to the three basic missions of the document, the restrictions of government are implied by the limits of what they can do. In other words, if the U.S. Constitution does NOT specifically enumerate something as a power of the government, or imply as necessary and proper, government is thereby restricted. This especially applies to actions by government that violates the rights of individuals.

The U.S. Constitution was never intended to be a list of government restrictions. If the U.S. Constitution did include such a list, then government could assume it would have certain powers that are not explicitly restricted by the Constitution.

The Modern Paradigm of Liberty

For example, there is no constitutional language restricting the U.S. government from relinquishing national sovereignty to an international socialist government, like the United Nations. Does the absence of this restriction imply its opposite? Absolutely not.

In short, the U.S. Constitution is a document that defines the shape and powers of the United States federal government and the rights of its citizens. It was never intended to be a restrictive document. In addition, the framers recognized the United States as a dynamic nation that expands and grows as well as subject to the control of the people. As a result, the final mission of U.S. Constitution is to grow and mature with the nation at the discretion and will of the people.

As a supplemental note to illustrate that the founders intended that individual liberties should be broadly construed, the 9th Amendment states that *"The enumeration in the Constitution, of certain rights, shall not be construed to deny or disparage others retained by the people."* The Constitution clearly facilitates the expansion of liberty. The only restrictions in the Constitution are Sections 9 and 10 of Article I, which include logical governmental/ administrative restrictions, such as a prohibition on individual states to enter into foreign treaties or mint currency.

The Confederate Battle Flag

On May 18, 2000, the Confederate Battle Flag saw its last day over the South Carolina State Capital building. The obvious question on everyone's mind should be "Why was there *any* official government sponsorship of the Confederate Battle Flag 135 years after the close of the Civil War?" Furthermore, how could any reasonable contemporary argument be made in its defense?

At the onset of the Civil War in the early days of 1861, numerous southern states of the establish American Federation publicly rejected the American Federal Government, the United States Constitution, renounced membership in the Union created by the founding fathers, and willfully took the treasonous position of taking up arms against the legitimate government and their fellow Americans. In short, they founded their entire movement on a set of principles and ideals that were by definition anti-American.

Sean McPhillips

There is no question in anyone's mind that the politics and actions of the Confederate States of America were those of a nation defining itself as an enemy of the United States of America. Fortunately for everyone, the South lost their insignificant rebellion and the Union remained intact, primarily due to the tenacity of President Lincoln.

Interestingly, the founding fathers considered a confederate model for the United States, and even initially employed one under the Articles of Confederation. However, they later rejected the confederate model because it was weak, flawed, and failed to establish sufficient cohesion of the member states. This is why they sunsetted the Articles of Confederation and established a federal model under the United States Constitution.

That stated, what's the deal with the Confederate Battle Flag? Given the above irrefutable facts, how can anyone who **claims** to be a patriotic American possibly defend public display and government sponsorship of the Confederate Battle Flag, particularly in a post-9/11 world where we need to emphasize national unity?

What defenders of the Confederate Battle Flag need to realize is that the Confederate States of America was politically no different than any other enemy of war in American history. To support the belief system of an enemy and defend its symbolic references in the American public is a deliberate slap in the face of the founding fathers and **real** Americans everywhere. Further, it would be tantamount to waving a flag signifying Saddam Hussein's Iraq, Al-Qaida's Afghanistan, or Nazi Germany.

True, in a free society, private people should be allowed to say and think whatever they like as long as they respect the liberties of others. If someone willfully chooses to engage in public *unpatriotic, anti-American* sentiment, such as waving the Confederate Battle Flag, I suppose that is their right. But they should also be aware that the public at-large knows precisely where their true loyalties lie.

Morals, Ethics and Government

Both sides of the Congressional isle like to preach about what is or is not morally and/or ethically acceptable behavior in the United States. Further, they like to dictate the benefits and the "importance" of family/traditional values and tie this back to the moral and ethical argument. While both sides differ on what is or is not considered to be moral and ethical, there is no question that these people are acting with the best of intentions, albeit subjectively based.

While they all operate under the assumption that they could impose generic morals, ethics and family values on Americans, no one seems to be asking whether or not they should. The U.S. Constitution clearly implies its three separate and distinct missions: define the structure of government, define the power of government, and define the rights of the people (see separate discussion). Of the numerous governmental powers defined by the Constitution, the power to define the morals and ethics of the United States is not one of them. Nor is it implied through the necessary and proper clause.

The fact is, when people want moral and ethical guidance, they seldom turn to governmental leaders for positive examples. The amount of immoral and unethical behavior that occurs by officials at all levels of government is both staggering and nauseating. In reality, when people want moral and ethical guidance, they often turn to non-secular sources, such as their faith.

Despite the recent questionable behavior of leaders in the Roman Catholic community, religions and their doctrines often define a basic code of ethical and moral conduct that many people embrace. Further, in a society that celebrates the freedom of religion, citizens have a diverse number of options to choose from, including no religion at all.

The question is, if someone has no religion, does that imply that he/she is not moral or ethical? Certainly not. While many belief systems based in religion include numerous subjective moral and ethical guidelines, they often also include what some might consider to be universally acceptable morals and ethics. Don't kill, don't lie, don't cheat, and don't steal are some of the common universal moral and ethical standards.

So how does this tie into government? When the framers conceived an ideal model of a free society, they did so based on a single principle, that everyone is equally entitled to life, liberty and the pursuit of happiness. Therefore, since this basic freedom principle defines the free society, what is implied is the acceptable behavior within that society. In short, as long as the exercise of an individual's freedoms do not infringe on the same rights entitled to all others in the free society, then their behavior should be acceptable by society. That is the only true limit on freedoms and liberties in a truly free society.

But on the individual level, the sources of one's morals and ethics boil down to one of three sources; themselves, their faith and/or their society. Faith is an established mechanism of morals and ethics as it is often backed by centuries of practice and official doctrine. But the faith-based morals and ethics argument fails when applied to those people outside the given faith. Faith-based morals and ethics imposed by society only apply to everyone if the society is officially one faith. But the United States is a multi-faith society so faith-based morals and ethics cannot be universally applied.

Society-based morals and ethics serves best as a general source of morals and ethics as society uses its experiences as the instrument for defining what is right and wrong. In this case, moral and ethical laws should be limited to those actions of people that infringe on the rights and liberties of others. But unfortunately, such morals and ethics are not all inclusive as they are limited towards intentional act that violate the freedoms of others.

Last, but not least is the individual himself. Ultimately, each individual gauges his/her moral and ethical judgments based on their own subjective opinions. An individual uses his/her own moral filter as the philosophical instrument to govern their own moral and ethical dilemmas on a case-by-case basis. One's moral filter is the product of their collective experiences, knowledge and understanding of the world around them. This culmination of wisdom includes, but is not limited to faith, personal experience, governance, and even the casual observation of others.

So, where should the line be drawn? The answer is clearly defined above. Society should only invoke laws that have moral implications in defense of the rights and liberties of its citizens, and that is it. The rest of one's subjective morals should be the product of their own vision quest.

If the individual chooses to make their faith the source of their remaining morals and ethics, then that is their right in a free society. However, if the individual chooses to use his/her personal experiences and observations as their source of morals and ethics, then that is also their right in a free society. No system is *objectively* right or wrong. But one thing is clear, it is wrong to force your subjective morals and ethics onto someone who does not embrace your belief system and source.

With respect to the promotion by government of so-called "family values," this ties back to the morals and ethics argument. It is not the right or responsibility of government to promote the notion of *traditional* family values as a good thing.

The reason is, this implies that the opposite of traditional family values is bad.

First of all, what is a *traditional* family? Is this a mother and father happily married, a few kids and a home with a white picket fence? Pragmatically, this is few and far between. With divorce, gay couple adoption, and unwed mothers at an all-time high, the so-called traditional family seems to be obscure and scarce. The fact is, there really is no universal definition of a family.

Further, there is no reason to assume that a child growing up in a traditional family will be better off than one in a non-traditional family. Even if statistics did favor the traditional family model, the reality is it boils down to the parenting. Kids need discipline, guidance, a good foundation, and an understanding of respect for their fellow man. Enter morals and ethics.

It is the responsibility of parents to calibrate their child's moral compass so that they can navigate through their lives with a reasonable basis of what is right and wrong. Religion is a common instrument that parents use and this is often an effective source at that. But whether or not parents choose to use a religion as the source of morals and ethics for their children, it is the parents' responsibility and **not** the government to educate their children on what is right and wrong.

World Government

There has been a lot of public discussion in recent years surrounding world governance and the fear for loss of American sovereignty. This discussion specifically focuses around the actions of the United Nations for the so-called "greater global good," and not necessarily in the best interests of free people.

When the United Nations can sit by idly and let tyrants like Saddam Hussein and Fidel Castro sit in power for decades and recognize them as equals with democratic nations, or oppressive governments like the Taliban/al-Qaida to exist, they send a clear message that they would be willing to let great civil rights atrocities occur under the false notion of world peace. As a result, the concept of world governance has been equated to the United Nations, and has received a bad rap for good reason.

Despite that the United States was one of the founding nations of the United Nations; the evolution of the United

Sean McPhillips

Nations to date has largely taken a European slant towards their brand of socialism. Yes, socialism. The United Nations has a track record of socialism that, if realized through to fruition, would undermine American sovereignty and erode the freedoms of American citizens.

Some of examples of threats to American liberties include:

- *Despite a prominent position on the United States' list of nations sponsoring terrorism, Syria won a seat on the U.N Security Council.*
- *Impose global population control standards and regulations.*
- *Disarming the people at-large so that only firearms owned by armies and law enforcement would be considered legal.*
- *Impose global education standards, which would likely shift children's perception of allegiance away from their home nation to the global "community," based on what the U.N. believes is right and wrong, and not what America believes.*
- *Deployment of U.S. armed forces on U.N.-sanctioned military missions.*
- *Initiatives to undermine private ownership of land because they believe it contributes to social injustice, necessitating public control.*

- *Impose international taxation to the United Nations (like the U.S. government doesn't already give the U.N. enough money and resources.)*
- *The International Criminal Court (ICC), which became a reality on July 1, 2002, would have the authority to prosecute American citizens. Further, American citizens would be denied right to habeas corpus, denied the right to confront your accuser, denied the right to a trial by jury of peers but instead a panel of six judges where only one judge can be American. Finally, ICC prosecutors will be allowed to present secret evidence to the judges, which violates the full disclosure of evidence we have in the United States.* [1]

For all these reasons, Americans need to be very skeptical of the intentions of the United Nations. The fears expressed by many Americans about this form of World Governance, including that of this author, are genuine and justifiably founded. But is world governance as a generic concept a bad idea in its entirety?

What if the world government model was one built on the principles of freedom, liberty, and federal republican democracy that the United States was built on? If that were the model, would world governance be a good idea then? Sure it would, and we would not have to compromise U.S. sovereignty to achieve it either.

As stated in an earlier discussion the model of the United States is not that of a typical nation, but rather it is a republican federation. This means that new nations/states can be incorporated into the United States. Ultimately, the complete expansion of this model could, in theory, include every nation of the world under the United States Constitution as the principle global governance document. We would then be the United States of Earth.

But perhaps for practical purposes, there would be an intermediary level of government, much like we currently have Federal, State, County, City, etc. Perhaps a practical application would be to have regional conferences, such as the United States of North America, the United States of South America, the United States of Africa, the United States of Europe, etc. Then, the global government would be the United Conferences of Earth, again all under the existing United States Constitution and basic principles of American liberty and freedom.

In addition, respectful use of the 10th Amendment by both the federal and state governments provides for a great deal of sovereignty to the individual states. Further, new states would have equal representation within the U.S. Congress as any other state would. Finally, the rights and privileges of United States citizenship would be extended to all citizens of new states as well as equal protection under the law.

So how would we achieve this? First, the United States should resign its membership in the United Nations. Then, Congress should pass something like a Federation Expansion Act. This Act would specifically allow for the inclusion of new states into the Union and define the five basic means by which states are incorporated.

Option 1: Voluntary Application

This is self explanatory. If a nation wishes to join the federation of the United States, they should be able to do so through a voluntary application process whereby they adopt the United States Constitution as their federal governance and modify all state and local law to be in compliance and not contradictory with federal law and the U.S. Constitution. Finally, they would recognize the United States federal government supreme to their own.

****

Option 2: Acquisition by Purchase

In 1803, the United States paid France $15 Million to acquire the Louisiana Purchase, a single business transaction, which doubled the size of the United States quite literally overnight. Today, thirteen states have been carved from the original Louisiana territory. If the United States wishes to grow, it should begin to leverage its affluence and procure new territories in a similar manner all over the world, even areas that may be undesirable and/or unpopulated.

Such areas could include: the Yukon Territory in Canada, the Amazon, the Congo, the Sahara Desert, Siberia, the Australian Outback, etc. Many of these places listed are sparsely populated, if at all. By acquiring these territories through legitimate business transactions, the United States would substantially increase in size and assert a permanent presence in more areas of the world.

This serves as an interest to help protect our country from foreign threats as well as brings a beacon of hope and freedom closer to those who need it most. The United States could also establish strategic military outposts in these areas. Further, the federal government could give businesses incentives to move to these new territories, which will help facilitate in the population of these areas.

Finally, these new territories could be populated and eventually become states if the Homestead Act were reinstated for these territories, which would give large pieces of land to anyone who is willing to work it. This worked well for early immigrants who settled out west in the continental United States, and there is no reason why it would not work here.

****

Option 3: Military Assistance and/or Liberation

The United States has often used a wealth of its resources to **assist** other nations. The particular concern is on those nations that solicit the assistance of the United States military. Let us examine Kuwait in early 1991. Kuwait was invaded and occupied by Iraq. The United States should have helped only on the condition that upon liberation of Kuwait, that Kuwait becomes a territory and ultimately a state of the United States. Had that happened in the early 1990s, the U.S. would have had a strong and permanent presence in the Middle East, easing the post-9/11 Afghan military campaigns and kept Saddam Hussein in check.

Operation Iraqi Freedom may not have needed to occur at all. But if it did and Iraq was liberated by the United States, the same rules would apply. The U.S. government could have liberated Iraq and then help establish them as a new state in our union with equal representation and protection under the law.

Upon the writing of this book, the United States has begun deployment of peace-keeping troops into Liberia to ease their Civil War and establish order as President Charles Taylor steps down. However, the United States should only continue these efforts in Liberia if they become a state. Ironically, Liberia is founded by freed American slaves, so there is even further legitimacy to this approach in Liberia as they are true distant relatives to the American Federation.

The United States has no obligation to assist any nation with military action and risk the lives of American soldiers. If any nation/state wants such assistance, then they should adopt our principles of liberty, freedom, and republican democracy. Therefore, they should become a member state of the United States.

****

Option 4: Other Assistance (ex. Financial)

Israel currently receives billions of dollars from the United States to prop them up in an area of the world that is completely hostile towards them. However, it is not the responsibility, obligation or duty of the United States to assist Israel at all. If Israel wants assistance from the United States to manage the Palestinian threat and/or protection from their Arab neighbors, then the United States should only do so if Israel agrees to become a state of the United States. Otherwise, they are on their own.

Fortunately, if the United States steps in, then the Israeli government and culture would likely remain mostly intact, since Israel is already a democracy. Plus, with the 10th Amendment,

Israel should otherwise retain a great deal of autonomy, providing that they do not contradict U.S. federal law.

****

Option 5: Annexation

What ever happened to the concept, "*to the victors go the spoils*?" Isn't this a basic right of victory, especially when an enemy attacked you? Yes, it is, especially in cases of self-defense. Nations have a basic right to protect themselves from hostile and aggressive forces, and if the hostile force is defeated, the defending nation has every right to be sure that the hostile force never attacks them again. By annexing enemy nations, establishing an American paradigm, enforcing American law, and spreading liberty and freedom, we would be eliminating that threat permanently. Plus, they would ultimately be treated as equals in our society.

Let us examine the post-9/11 situation in Afghanistan. The Taliban and al-Qaida, which were the controlling interests and government of Afghanistan, were directly responsible for the attacks on September 11, 2001. This justifies the United States to take military action against them. Upon completion of the campaign, the U.S. helped them establish a provisional government and ultimately will back out of Afghanistan with the hopes that the Afghanis will build a nation based on freedom,

Sean McPhillips

liberty and democracy, and be a long-term friend and ally of the United States. Yeah, right.

But why should the U.S. mission end there? The fact that they attacked the U.S. gives us every right to make sure that it does not happen again. Upon completion of military efforts, the U.S. should establish an appointed U.S. interim government. This interim government would enforce all federal U.S. laws that apply to any non-state territory within the U.S. Then, this interim government would assist the State of Afghanistan to create a State Constitution, much like any other state in the Union, where the State Constitution does not conflict with the U.S. Constitution.

Upon ratification of the state constitution, the U.S. would sponsor free, honest and fair elections for the State of Afghanistan. Once the government for the State of Afghanistan is represented in a democratic paradigm, the interim U.S. appointed government would then take a back seat, but remain present to insure that federal laws are still enforced. Finally, after many years, the State of Afghanistan will be formally indoctrinated into the United States as a State of the Union, with all rights, freedoms, liberties, and privileges extended to the state and citizens therein.

In short, we would destroy the original, oppressive government built on fear and tyranny, and replace it with the most mature and successful model of liberty and freedom in the world. Furthermore, this would permanently eliminate the threat that would otherwise continue to fester and ultimately jeopardize the United States again.

So, is this such a bad thing? The people of Afghanistan would be as free as people can be in the world and not fear the actions of an oppressive minority. Perhaps this is what the United States should have done to Japan in 1945. We could only imagine how much different the Korean War, the Vietnam War and the rest of the Cold War might have been had we executed such policy.

****

But there are those who would question that these actions are also oppressive, and arguably the actions of conquerors. Not true. The ultimate mission for each of these state conversions should be to establish them as free U.S. states with all the rights and liberties as any other state, and provide U.S. citizenship to all members of that former nation/state with all the rights and liberties of any other U.S. citizen. With that end in mind, there really is no downside.

Furthermore, this is consistent with the vision of the founding fathers. On the back of the U.S. dollar bill, there are two Latin phrases surrounding the pyramid on the left side. They state **"Annuit Coeptis, Novus Ordo Seclorum."** The closest literal English translation is "favor the undertaking, new order of the world." This is a clear indication by the founders that they intended the ideals of liberty and freedom by which the United States was founded, to be the basis for providing a new vision for the whole world.

The concern that we would be disrupting or damaging other cultures is also false, as any and all cultures and religions can thrive in the United States federation, providing one religious and/or cultural belief system is not allowed to dominate through formal actions of government.

Finally, people who would criticize this model are clearly putting the interests of oppressive governments over the basic human rights and liberties of people. What it boils down to is a question of which is more sovereign; a nation or the people?

---

[1] *http://www.getusout.com/ (all notes are paraphrased from this web site)*

Contingency Government for Disaster Recovery

Throughout the history of the American Presidency, there have been several instances where the President was unable to complete his term and had to be succeeded by the Vice President. This has occurred several times, of the most notable were those involving assassination.

The 25th Amendment to the United States Constitution formally defines the succession of the Presidency to fall to the Vice President in the event that the President was to leave office for any reason prior to completion of his term. The official succession thereafter includes, in order, The Speaker of the House of Representatives, The President Pro Tempore of the Senate, The Secretary of State and then the remaining members of The Cabinet. This order of succession has served the United States well, until now.

Sean McPhillips

In the wake of September 11th, 2001, Americans were quickly reminded that there are real threats in this world to the American people and our way of life. As onlookers of the terrorists attacks in Israel and considering the fact that terrorist sleeper cells likely exist in every major city of the United States, the question of another major act of terrorism is not a question of "*if*" but "**when**."

This threat becomes more prominent when we consider nations like North Korea and Iran attempting to build and/or acquire weapons of mass destruction. Further, add the fact that the collapse of the former Soviet Union left countless nuclear warheads in their peripheral and impoverished territories, many of which are now unaccounted for. Considering all this, the threat of nuclear terrorism on American soil becomes a very real one.

So, if a terrorist wanted to do the most damage, physically, emotionally, and organizationally, they would likely detonate a nuclear device in Washington, D.C. somewhere between the White House and the Capital Building. This would completely decimate the formal federal government of the people because the President, Vice President, The Cabinet, The Speaker of the House of Representatives, The President Pro Tempore of the Senate, and the vast majority of both Houses of Congress would all perish simultaneously. An ideal time to strike would be during the State of the Union because they are all in one location at the same time and the whole nation is watching.

The Modern Paradigm of Liberty

The question is: what is the constitutional provision if they all were to simultaneously perish? The answer is **there isn't**. So what would happen? While each state in the Union is self sufficient enough to function on their own if needed, there would be no formal federal authority to maintain cohesion of the states in the Union, with one exception.

The only formal federally controlled organization capable of immediately stepping up to the leadership challenge during this crisis scenario, establish order and maintain a chain of command would be the United States Military. In an instant, the United States would become a military dictatorship.

Personally, this author would like to believe that, under these circumstances, the United States Military will act in the best interest of the American people, their liberties and freedoms, and the United States Constitution, but there is no guarantee or protection against tyranny under these circumstances. Furthermore, if a rouge U.S. General wanted to seize power, he could do so in this exact same way and blame it on terrorism. Who would question it?

So what do we do? Simple, we need a contingency plan for disaster recovery assuming the worst could happen, which would need to be an amendment to the United States Constitution for it to be official. The solution is right before our eyes and almost completely organized already: **The National Governors Association**.

Sean McPhillips

The National Governors Association (NGA) is, obviously, an association where the governors from all 50 states gather to discuss issues that affect all states in the Union. This forum has historically served the Governors well and continues to be used to raise and address the issues facing the American people in a non-legislative venue.

The forum of the NGA provides the governors with a great deal of freedom to discuss the critical topics and represent the interests of their states to their peers. However, the NGA has no formal legal power, nor does it have any constitutionally defined function or authority at the federal level. But with an amendment to the U.S. Constitution, that could change.

The proposal is this; should a disaster befall the federal government and they all perish as described above, the NGA should immediately be considered the **Interim United States Government**, where the President/Chairman of the NGA would immediately become the **Interim United States President** and the Vice President/Vice Chairman of the NGA, would immediately become the **Interim United States Vice President**, both of which would possess all the executive authority empowered to the President and Vice President under normal circumstances.

The remaining governors would all be the single representatives of the people in their states and serve as the **Interim Congress**. All Lieutenant Governors would assume the role of **Acting Governor** for their respective states. For the two governors now serving as the Interim President and Interim Vice President, they would each have the authority to appoint their replacement designees in the Interim Congress. This would quickly reestablish both an Interim Executive Branch and Interim Legislative Branch of the Federal Government.

The first action of the Interim Government would be to triage the crisis situation and reestablish the government as one of the people, by the people and for the people. Then, special elections should commence immediately to return the government to the traditional model as prescribed by the United States Constitution. After the traditional government is restored, the NGA would relinquish their authority as the Interim Government.

This model would insure that there will always be a government consisting of elected officials and would never allow for the United States Military to ever be in a position of total authority as they would always be subject to the civilian authority. Furthermore, this would be a constitutional weapon in the *War on Terror* as this would minimize the impact of such an act of terrorism. Without this disaster recovery plan, the vision of liberty and freedom conceived by the founders over 225 years ago could vanish is a flash of light and in the blink of an eye.

Volunteer Marshal Corps

In the wake of 9/11 there was an overwhelming outcry for an increased level of security to ensure protection of the American people from any enemies foreign or domestic. Of course, everyone was concerned about when and where the next act of terrorism was going to be and in what form that act would be in.

As a result, the Federal Government created the Transportation Safety Administration, Sky Marshals, the Department of Homeland Security, and even the "Patriot" Act. While all of these provide some illusion of security, we need to ask ourselves what the everyday American citizen can do to take an active role in defending our nation and what could the Federal Government do to facilitate this.

We need to remember that this is not the first time in American history when terrorist attacks happened in our backyards without warning. During the early years of this nation when the West was largely unsettled, remote communities were subject to surprise attacks from Native Americans who weren't too happy about these new settlements encroaching on their territories. Among many other reasons, the real threat of surprise domestic attacks was one of the driving forces behind the right to keep and bear arms.

The Second Amendment to the United States Constitution states that a *well regulated Militia, being necessary to the security of a free State, the right of the people to keep and bear Arms, shall not be infringed.* One of the reasons for this is to empower the people as citizen soldiers and defenders of liberty whenever liberty is threatened. I think it is safe to say that with the reality of terrorist sleeper cells on American soil and planes crashing into skyscrapers, that liberty is being threatened. So how can the citizenry at-large defend liberty and how can the Federal Government facilitate them?

There are those who believe that the scope and limit of the Second Amendment begins and ends with law enforcement agencies and the National Guard. While this discussion is not a debate on the Second Amendment in general, it is important to point out that the militia as defined by federal law is as follows:

Title 10 Chapter 13, 10 USC Sec. 311:

(a) The militia of the United States consists of all able-bodied males at least 17 year of age and, except as provided in

section 313 of title 32, under 45 years of age who are, or who have made a declaration of intention to become, citizens of the United States and of female citizens of the United States who are commissioned officers of the National Guard.

(b) The classes of the militia are –

1. *the organized militia, which consists of the National Guard and the Naval Militia; and*
2. *the unorganized militia, which consists of the members of the militia who are not members of the National Guard or the Naval Militia.*[1]

Now, given the language of the Second Amendment, the Federal definition of the militia, and the contemporary needs of applying them both given the rise in crime and potential terrorist threats, what can we do to satisfy the real security needs of America, while respecting individual liberties and empowering the citizenry? The answer is to create a *Volunteer Marshal Corps*.

The Federal Government should establish a Volunteer Marshal Corps where law-abiding citizens would be allowed to obtain formal training equal to that of a Federal Officer, such as an FBI Special Agent. Upon successful completion of their training, they would be issued a badge and empowered with the authority to enforce the law as any other law enforcement officer would anywhere within the jurisdiction of the United States. More importantly, upon completion of their training, they would return to their normal lives in their normal profession and would otherwise not be government employees.

However, should a Volunteer Marshal witness a crime in progress, he/she would have full law enforcement authority to intercede. A Volunteer Marshal would also have the authority to assist any level of law enforcement as needed. They could serve as Sky Marshals on any flight they travel on, especially if they work in a profession that requires a lot of travel. Most importantly, in the event of a major national crisis, such as 9/11, Volunteer Marshals could be immediately notified and summoned to the crisis location to provide supplemental assistance.

Further, since Volunteer Marshals would have the law-enforcement authority of Federal Agents, they would be authorized to carry firearms either open or concealed anywhere within U.S. jurisdiction. Plus, if the Volunteer Marshal decides to pursue a career as a Federal Agent, this training would qualify as credit.

In summary, there are countless thousands of patriotic Americans who would be willing to serve this country in this capacity, should the option be available. A citizen should not have to give up several years of their life to serve in the military in order to serve their country, nor should he/she have to give up a lucrative career to take a government law enforcement position at a fraction of their previous salary.

A government paycheck is really the only difference between a Volunteer Marshal and a Federal Agent. If the Federal Government is genuinely concerned about homeland security, they should do everything possible to empower the law-abiding citizenry to ensure that the homeland is secure.

[1] *http://www4.law.cornell.edu/uscode/10/311.html*

Capital Punishment

When Timothy McVeigh was put to death, how many Americans lost sleep? Probably very few. The reality is there are some criminal acts that are just so heinous that even the ultimate sentence does not fit the crime. So, should we set aside capital punishment?

The United States has received a great deal of criticism over the years from our European *allies* about the use of capital punishment. The so-called barbarism of capital punishment is often equated to the actions of Third World nations. Some nations have even refused to extradite criminals to the United States or provide critical intelligence on the War on Terror because of our capital punishment policy. In the international arena, employing capital punishment has not worked to our advantage, nor has it domestically.

Crime statistics keep going up, including violent crime. Unfortunately, there is no hard evidence to suggest that capital punishment reduces crime or saves society money. Further, there is always the smallest chance that an innocent person might be executed, although very unlikely with the existence of DNA testing. So, what should we do about capital punishment?

Fox News Analyst Bill O'Reilly has suggested numerous times on his popular program *The O'Reilly Factor* that the United States should do away with capital punishment but set up a labor camp in the middle of Alaska for all prisoners sentenced to life in prison without parole. When this author first heard this, it reminded me of a thought I had years earlier in a similar context.

I agree that a labor camp in lieu of capital punishment would be better, but let's take it to the next level by using a lesson from history. Centuries ago, much of this world was settled by Europeans as a product of deploying penal colonies. It worked then, there's no reason why it won't work now.

Mr. O'Reilly is on the right track, but he is not going far enough. This author suggests that instead of sending them to Alaska, we send them to Antarctica. The United States should set up a penal colony on Antarctica and send all eligible prisoners there to *work the land*. They could dig all the ice off of Antarctica, or at least enough to build the colony. Then, they could begin building a city or a military base down there.

Think about it, there would be little need for security or jail cells or any other security measure. Plus, they are providing a societal good as they would be taking a hostel wasteland and making it habitable for their civilized countrymen. In time (and a very long time) Antarctica would no longer be the wasteland it currently is, but a living and growing community.

But why end there? By the time the prisoners finish with Antarctica, the U.S. space program would have probably advanced to the point where Lunar and/or Martian colonization will become a reality. Employ the same solution. Send the prisoners to the Moon and to Mars to begin building the first colonies in space.

This should satisfy anyone who objects to the notion of capital punishment. Second, anyone sentenced will still remain alive in the event that they are later proven innocent. Third, the sentence is so severe and undesirable that it would substantially deter criminals.

Finally, it would disconnect prisoners completely from the outside world, so that they cannot smuggle in drugs or other contraband. Further, many prisoners still manage to maintain an active role in their criminal enterprises. This solution would completely remove them from the equation.

In any case, until a sentence more undesirable then death can be implemented, capital punishment seems to be the most severe sentence the American criminal justice system has to offer. Unless we unconstitutionally reinstate torture or other cruel and unusual punishment instead of the above suggestion, we will have to accept the reality that violent crime will continue to rise with no end in site.

Accountability of Parole Boards

With the existence of television dramas like *Law & Order*, the layman has an opportunity to peak into the criminal justice system and see some of its inner workings. One of these inner workings is the parole board. Sentences with parole conditions are usually handed down with both a minimum and maximum time in jail, where the prisoner is eligible for parole after the minimum time is served. For example, if a prisoner is sentenced to 8⅓ to 25 years, then he/she would be eligible for parole in 100 months.

Parole boards are used if a criminal sentence allows for a prisoner to be set free before completion of the maximum term of his/her sentence. The parole board gets to decide if the prisoner is fit to return to society.

But what accountability do parole boards have for their decision? What if they release a prisoner prior to the completion of the maximum jail time in the prisoner's sentence and then the prisoner commits another crime? Basically, there is no accountability on the part of the parole board.

In theory, a parole board could release a prisoner simply because of political pressure associated with the prisoner's case, the politics of the administration, or even overcrowded jails. This is outrageous and something needs to be done.

Assume a prisoner convicted of killing someone (murder, manslaughter, etc.) is paroled before the completion of his/her maximum sentence. If this prisoner violates parole by criminally victimizing someone else at some point before the completion of his/her maximum jail sentence would have been, then the parole board clearly released the prisoner prematurely and should be in some way held accountable. Accountability should be in either pecuniary damages via tort suits, criminal prosecution of parole board members, or both.

It is understandable that parole boards cannot predict the future and they have to make their recommendations based on what limited information they have before them. But, that does not excuse the fact that there are so many repeat offenders who break the law while they are on parole, and in some cases kill.

If parole boards were held to serious accountability standards by the people, instead of the immunity they currently enjoy, then perhaps they would begin to act more so in the best interest of the people to whom they are supposed to be serving, instead of serving politics.

This is not to suggest that the prisoners should serve more than their maximum term on their sentence, but rather to serve more of their existing sentence by reducing their chances of parole eligibility, which minimizes the likelihood of a career criminal. Ultimately, this should have a significant impact on lowering crime because substantially fewer prisoners would be paroled and any crimes they would have otherwise committed have been subsequently and proactively avoided.

Circumventing Due Process

Many people believe, rather naively, that all Americans are entitled to basic due process standards in any adjudication proceeding. We see it on cop shows all the time when suspects are Mirandized with "You have the *right* to remain silent, you have the *right* to an attorney, etc."

But do you believe that you always have these rights under *all* circumstances? Can you be charged with violating the law, convicted and sentenced all without access to these rights? Yes, you can, and most people don't even realize it. This situation occurs when a person is charged with violating administrative law. That is, law that was established as a rule created by an administrative agency.

But the U.S. Constitution does not specifically define the authority to create any administrative agencies. So, where does government get the authority to create administrative agencies? Virtually all administrative agencies owe their existence to the "necessary and proper clause" in Article I, Section 8 of the U.S. Constitution. State Constitutions usually employ similar principles.

Basically, Article I, Section 8 of the U.S. Constitution enumerates the powers of the federal government. The very last clause states that Congress has the power "*to make all laws which shall be necessary and proper for carrying into execution the foregoing powers, and all other powers vested by this Constitution in the government of the United States, or in any department or officer thereof.*"

This means that Congress has the power to create any laws they feel are necessary and proper to execute an enumerated power. As illustrated in an earlier discussion, Congress has the enumerated power to "lay and collect taxes" but does not have the enumerated power to create the Internal Revenue Service. However, the existence of the IRS is deemed *necessary and proper* for the function of managing taxation in the United States.

So, since the existence of all administrative agencies is implied and not expressly enumerated, so are their powers. In short, they enjoy being subject to a less stringent due process model. That means the rights that you expect to receive in a criminal prosecution do not apply when you are charged with violating administrative law.

And where does administrative law come from? Well, the legislature has the constitutional authority to create the administrative agency. In doing so, the legislature delegates rule-making authority to the administrative agency. After that, the administrative agency defines their set of rules, which impact the population and have the effect of law.

Further, administrative agencies consist entirely of appointed officials. In other words, they are not representative of the people. These people are unelectable, unaccountable and, in many cases, irremovable by the people and answer only to the Executive Branch.

Even further, the administrative agencies get to define their own rules with the effect of law, and in many cases enforce them through *their* adjudication process. Under the U.S. Constitution, no body/branch of government can both create laws and then enforce them. That violates the separation of powers. Somehow, administrative agencies have weaseled their legal way around the separation of powers embodied in the first three Articles in the U.S. Constitution.

Finally, since administrative agencies are under the protection of the Executive Branch, they are subjected to a less stringent due process model. That means a person can be charged with violating these laws, subjected to a tribunal and denied a trial by jury, denied counsel, and even be forced to provide self-incriminating testimony. All of these rights are guaranteed to anyone in the criminal adjudication process.

So, someone charged with multiple homicides has more rights and protection under the law then someone contesting motor vehicle revocation, condemned land for public use, or tax evasion. This is outrageous. And, more specifically, most people are not even aware this exists until it happens to them.

What concerns this author even more is that since administrative agencies are extensions of the Executive Branch, they can be used/abused by those in power as an attempt to stifle those who criticize them. Case and point, Fox News Analyst Bill O'Reilly repeatedly criticized the Clinton Administration on his show *The O'Reilly Factor* and coincidently was subjected to tax audits three years in a row.

Similar coincidences have occurred for people like Paula Jones and Juanita Broderick, both of whom accused President Clinton of sexual misconduct. For those who have never been through an audit, it is the financial equivalent of a "complete proctology examination," as Jerry Seinfeld would put it.

Recently in 1998, the IRS changed their tune about the burden of proof. The revision in 1998 shifted the burden of proof onto the IRS instead of the taxpayer. That's good, right? But before the change, the burden of proof was **on** the taxpayer! That's right, if you were charged with violating their laws, you had to prove your innocence! What ever happened to "innocent until proven guilty" where the burden of proof was on The People? Remember, this applies to any Administrative Agency, as they can shift the burden of proof on the accused instead of The People where it should be.

The Modern Paradigm of Liberty

Despite the significant violations of citizens' rights, we cannot expect government to radically change overnight to ensure that the constitutional rights of the citizens are protected in every venue. Contemporary government got this way gradually over the past 150 years or so. But, that does not mean we, as Americans, have to take it or like it.

The abuses of authority by administrative agencies have been circumventing the U.S. Constitution and our rights for too long. It is time we take a stand and hold them accountable any way we can. Putting pressure on our legislators and executives should do the trick. After all, they finally shifted the burden of proof from the taxpayer to the IRS, so we know we can effect positive change.

Special Note: *This discussion was partially inspired by the following web site:*
http://www.we-caire-nh.org/

Case Law Review

Most levels of government within the United States are segregated into three separate branches, Executive, Legislative and Judicial. The separation of powers guaranteed by the founders in the United States Constitution is intentionally constructed to prevent any one branch from asserting authority over the other two. This is pivotal to the success of the American republic as power in the United States is deliberately distributed in an effort to ultimately protect the people from tyranny. But do the courts have too much power?

The judicial system in the U.S. is built on adversarial legalism. That is, we have a plaintiff and a defendant who are treated equally and objectively in the eyes of the court, specifically the judge. The judge serves as the arbitrator over the adversarial process and the counsel for both parties argue their respective cases wielding the law as their weapon in an effort to be victorious.

But the challenge for any attorney is to have a complete knowledge of the entire body of law, specifically as it relates to the case they are presenting. Much of this law exists in the form of case law, which is the product of judicial rulings in previous trials. Given that case law literally dates back to the founding of the nation, having a complete knowledge of all previous case law is impossible.

This is particularly more difficult where case laws contradict one another. This is further complicated by the fact that previous case law rulings are the micro decisions made based on the circumstances of specific cases, and not macro laws specifically intended for society at large.

In addition, the judge in his/her courtroom and chambers has a great deal of discretion with respect to their rulings. In short, the judge subjectively decides the interpretation of the law, swings the gavel, and their decision becomes law unless their ruling is overturned by a higher court or an act of the legislature. By design, this places too much authority on a single individual (or small group of people, such as an appellate court). In many cases, these justices are appointed and are minimally accountable to the people.

When we think of the term "law maker" we envision members of the legislature and not judges. Judges are enforcers of the law and not the law makers. But case law is often used as an end-run around the legislative process. A popular example is Roe vs. Wade. Here, the U.S. Supreme

Court ruled that Abortion is a Constitutional Right of women, even though abortion is not specifically enumerated or implied by the U.S. Constitution. With that ruling, abortion became legal.

Legalized abortion was never subjected to the traditional law making process of a bill proposed by the House of Representatives, Senate, or the President. Instead, a gavel swung at it became law, period. The voice of the people through their representation never had a chance to make the argument or present the discussion for debate prior to it becoming law. Instead, it has become an after-the-fact debate that has been raging for over 30 years.

So what can we do? Since judges at all levels of government are not law makers by design, but arbitrators instead, they should retain their discretion on a case by case basis. But the historical body of case law should be collectively compiled, categorized, and generalized to apply to all cases relevant to their categories and not specific to individual cases. Then, these should be presented to the legislative body in a bill, or series of bills, for legislative review and ultimately submitted and passed through the traditional law making process.

When these bills are passed, all previous case law prior to the beginning of the case law review would be superseded by the laws enumerated in the new bills. This should be a process that is repeated in regular intervals, such as every ten years.

Once a policy such as this in imposed, any case law that precedes the last case law review becomes null and void for all future court cases. This both simplifies the legal process and returns an enormous amount of the law making process to the people and not the judges.

Without such a review, the courts will continue to circumvent the legislative process and the mountain of case law will continue to pile up with no end in site. Further, all this occurs without the approval of the people through a democratic process. It is about time that the people stand up to the arrogance of the courts and reclaim some of the power that they have. It is the people in a free society, and not the courts, that are sovereign. Therefore, the people as a whole get to decide what the laws are in society, and not a handful of justices with their own subjective agendas.

The Basic Flaws of Criminal Adjudication

One of the treasured rights of the American criminal justice system is the notion that all defendants are innocent until proven guilty. Obviously, this puts the burden of proof on The People. While other nations like Japan have the inverse, where defendants are guilty by accusation from the state and therefore have to prove their innocence, the American method of criminal adjudication affords a defendant every opportunity to protect their liberties and freedom.

However, while this is part of the foundation of our criminal justice system, there are two key flaws in such a system. First, in our criminal justice system, the jury is **supposed** to be the finder of facts when handing down a verdict. Before a jury can conclude on the facts, **all** the facts need to be presented to them. This brings up the admissibility of evidence. If evidence is acquired by illegal means, this evidence can be deemed inadmissible and therefore never presented to the jury for consideration.

For example: A videotape exists showing the defendant committing the crime. The prosecutor, defense council and the judge all view the videotape, therefore all three parties know for a fact that the defendant committed the crime. However, the tape was acquired through an invalid search warrant and a defense motion to suppress is granted.

The question: How can a jury, who are defined by law to be the finders of facts, accurately conclude on the case when they are deprived some facts relevant to the case as a matter of law? Further, in this same example, the defense can still argue **alternate** theories of the crime which divert the blame away from the defendant and onto someone else, even though the defense council, the prosecutor and the judge all know for a fact that such alternate theory is not true. In this author's opinion, this is tantamount to suborning perjury as is falsely represents the facts and intentionally misleads the jury with suggestive untruths.

The second major flaw in the American criminal justice system is the notion of innocent until proven guilty, which allows for a guilty man to go free, particularly in light of the previous argument. The question: What is the difference between Innocent and Not Guilty? In a legal context, they are the same. But in reality, they have very different meanings. Innocent means that the defendant did not commit the crime.

Not Guilty means that the evidence presented before the jury was insufficient for the jury to conclude beyond a reasonable doubt that the defendant committed the crime.

In short, innocent means, "you didn't do it", while not guilty means, "you might have done, but we couldn't prove it at this time". That is a significant difference between the two. When you factor the previous flaw and couple this with the shenanigans of defense attorneys, many truly guilty people can escape justice unfairly, especially when the defense has the financial resources to acquire premium council.

For justice to work in a free society, ultimately, the truth should prevail. That means the innocent should stay free, the guilty should be punished and the truth should never be hidden from anyone. While the acquisition of the inadmissible evidence might be illegal, that illegal action does not make the evidence any less true.

Since the evidence communicates the truth, it should be presented to jury regardless of how it was acquired. However, if such policy did exist, the enforcement branch of justice would often violate the law and rights of individuals to acquire such evidence in an effort to assist prosecution.

The compromise is this, the evidence should be admissible, but those who acquired said evidence illegally should be reprimanded with the same zeal as any other criminal activity. There actions should be public record and the people should hold them accountable. While we can't empower law enforcement to violate the rights of people, we shouldn't allow the guilty to go free on a technicality.

Further, a not-guilty verdict protects a defendant from double jeopardy. While protection from double jeopardy is essential to our system, it does still allow the truly guilty to walk free. The solution should be as follows, instead of innocent until proven guilty, the defendant should be not guilty until proven guilty or innocent, where the burden of proof of guilt is still on the prosecution but the burden of proof of innocence is on the defense. In this model the following would apply:

- a *guilty* verdict should remain as it currently is, that the defendant committed the crime as a fact of law.
- a *not-guilty* verdict should serve the equivalent of a mistrial and the defendant should be released. However, it should also provide the prosecution with one more opportunity to retry the case. Basically, it would be the jury's decision that there is insufficient evidence to convict, but there exist sufficient evidence to continue investigation. Thus, the jury would provide the prosecution with one more opportunity to make their case. It would then be at the discretion of the prosecution to proceed only once again. Further, if the jury hands down a not guilty verdict, then those damaged by the actions of the defendant can file civil

suit for damages. Case and point: The O.J. Simpson criminal and civil trials.

- an *innocent* verdict is the jury asserting that the defendant did not commit the crime as a fact of law. If the jury issues an *innocent* verdict, then jeopardy should be immediately attached as it is currently for *not guilty* verdicts. This option would provide the defense with legal grounds to file tort suit against the prosecution (*The People*) for defamation of character, lost wages, attorney's fees, etc. In short, this will provide the truly innocent with protection from malicious prosecution and a means to hold *The People* accountable for their otherwise negligent act of wrongful prosecution. Further, an innocent verdict should also insolate the defendant from any civil suit relating to the crime. For example, if O.J. Simpson were to be found innocent as defined above, any subsequent civil suit would have been disallowed.

Will these changes ever come to pass, who knows? The fact is, the United States still has the best criminal justice system in the world. But the system isn't perfect. These alternatives provide for improvements in the system to further protect the innocent, punish the guilty, and keep the law enforcers honest, i.e., enforcing accountability all around. Without these kinds of changes, the cracks and flaws in our system will continue to exist and erode away the confidence of the American people in the effectiveness of the system to exact justice as well as serve and protect the people.

Atheism versus Socialism

The ignorance of people with respect to religious and governmental beliefs has never been more evident with the assumption that atheism equals socialism/communism, and vice versa. This is a myth that is often perpetuated by a handful of self-serving conservatives and believed by the ignorant masses.

In truth, the religious beliefs of Atheism and the governmental beliefs of Socialism & Communism are separate and distinct by definition. According to Merriam-Webster's Dictionary, the definitions for each are as follows:

Atheism: **a:** a disbelief in the existence of deity **b:** the doctrine that there is no deity.[1]

Socialism: **1:** any of various economic and political theories advocating collective or governmental ownership and administration of the means of production and distribution of goods, **2 a:** a system of society or group living in which there is no private property **b:** a system or condition of society in which the means of production are owned and controlled by the state, **3:** a stage of society in Marxist theory transitional between capitalism and communism and distinguished by unequal distribution of goods and pay according to work done.[2]

Communism: **1 a:** a theory advocating elimination of private property **b:** a system in which goods are owned in common and are available to all as needed, **2** *capitalized* **a:** a doctrine based on revolutionary Marxian socialism and Marxism-Leninism that was the official ideology of the U.S.S.R. **b:** a totalitarian system of government in which a single authoritarian party controls state-owned means of production **c:** a final stage of society in Marxist theory in which the state has withered away and economic goods are distributed equitably **d:** communist systems collectively.[3]

If you look at these definitions, you can clearly see that Atheism does not imply Socialism or Communism in any way, or vice versa. So, how did these ever get entangled and why do so many people believe that one implies the other?

When the Union of Soviet Socialist Republics (a misnomer in itself) formalized their government, they did so in a socialist paradigm to ultimately aspire towards pure communism. Since socialism and communism ultimately thrive on depriving individual freedoms and liberties for the benefit of the commune, including that of religious freedom, they needed to

The Modern Paradigm of Liberty

make a formal stance on religion for the *good of society as a whole*.

Since religious beliefs vary widely from faith to faith, sect to sect, person to person, choosing one religion would not be practical. But abolishing religion altogether was practical and formally possible. Abolishment allowed for the USSR to force everyone into the commune by depriving their individual free expression. So, the official religious position of formal socialism/communism became atheism.

But does that mean that everyone who is a socialist/communist is an atheist? **No**. The fact is, the USSR could have been socialist/communist and forced a religious edict on the people for a particular faith. Here, the same rules of socialism/communism would still apply. The only difference would be an official religion of the commune, requiring everyone to embrace it under penalty of law. Today, people can still believe in the socialist/communist principle, but also be devout believers in their faiths.

So, does this mean that everyone who is an atheist is also a socialist/communist? **No**. Atheists exist here in the United States and represent every part of the political spectrum from very conservative to very liberal. They simply believe there is no God, period. A belief that there is no God has no bearing on political beliefs of anyone, including abortion, gun rights, or system of government.

This notion that atheism and socialism/communism are synonymous is utter nonsense perpetuated by the ignorant and those with manipulative religious agendas. This is not to be construed that all people of faith subscribe to such nonsense. Rather, a small minority sustain this myth in an effort to confuse the uninformed to further their subjective hidden agenda. That is an abuse of both religious freedom and free speech granted each of us in a free society.

Finally, the free expression of religious beliefs or any other beliefs can only exist in a free society. Nobody, for any reason, should be deprived the practice of their beliefs, have them infringed upon or formally undermined by the governing authority, regardless of what belief system they embrace. More discussion on the mutual exclusivity of religion and government can be found in a later discussion.

---

[1] *http://www.m-w.com/cgi-bin/dictionary, search word "Atheism".*
[2] *http://www.m-w.com/cgi-bin/dictionary, search word "Socialism".*
[3] *http://www.m-w.com/cgi-bin/dictionary, search word "Communism".*

Marriage versus Civil Unions

What does the word marriage conjure up in your mind? What does it mean to you? What role does marriage play in our society? These are questions the answers to which we take for granted. But do we always view marriage in the same light? This becomes more of an issue as the gay community poses their stance that same-sex couples should have the right to get *married*.

To appease those in government who consider marriage to be a sacred institution, the semantics of the nomenclature has renamed same-sex marriage to be *civil unions*, but would retain all the same legal benefits of marriage. This discussion should raise the obvious next question. What is the **real** difference between a marriage and a civil union?

The image of marriage in a civil context is quite simple. Legally, the lives of the two people are joined in a mutually equal and beneficial partnership. This legal partnership defines certain rights of each party with respect to the other, as well as additional benefits and protections under the law. Even the dissolution of the partnership requires legal intervention to divide assets and provide for mutual agreement of the partners to discontinue operating as a partnership.

The historical image of marriage in a family context is also quite simple. The man and the woman get married for the purpose of sharing their lives together. Most couples hope to raise children, provide for their offspring, raise them in a nurturing environment, etc. Further, there is also an implied sexual relationship between the two partners. Most of these family-based characteristics are relatively universal across the marriage concept.

The image of marriage in a religious context is also reasonably simple, but varies subjectively based on the religious beliefs of the faith. The various faiths that endorse marriage often have specific guidelines for qualifying the marriage, as well as the roles and responsibilities of the partners and offspring. Further, the religious aspect is often very closely related to the family aspect.

The above clearly illustrates that there are both legal and non-legal contexts to marriage. But, when we suggest the word *marriage*, we assume that all of the above apply. That stated, it becomes evident why those who hold strong traditional religious values would be opposed to legalizing same-sex marriage.

So, if accepting marriage for same-sex couples is a problem for some people, is there an alternative to marriage that satisfies both groups? This is where the concept of the civil union comes in. But that also raises a different question; does government have the **authority** to solemnize a marriage at all?

Solemnizing a marriage implies the celebration of a **religious** rite. While legally, government should have the authority to unite people together for the purpose of a mutual partnership (which occurs in business situations all the time); does government have any religious authority to perform the sacred act of a **marriage** ceremony? Further, if government does have religious authority over marriage, then wouldn't that violate the separation of church and state?

Perhaps the best way to illustrate this is through analogy. The difference between a marriage and a civil union is the same as the difference between a Jewish Bris and a circumcision. One has specific religious significance while the other has a utilitarian societal function.

A violation of the separation argument becomes most problematic for those who wish to protect their religious autonomy from government. This becomes a problem for the religious individuals because if government has the authority to solemnize a marriage, then by an act of the legislature or the courts in favor same-sex marriage, governments can then require that all religions recognize same-sex marriage by making discrimination against same-sex couples illegal. This is the most likely reason why religious groups are so opposed to legalizing same-sex marriage, and it is a good reason.

So what is the alternative? Well, since the legal and non-legal aspects of a marriage are separate, distinct and mutually exclusive, they should be separated under the law. Government should only have the authority to enforce the legal context of marriage and not posses any authority of solemnizing marriage. This means that marriage in the non-legal context can be subjectively recognized by the religions entirely at their discretion. For example, if Roman Catholics do not wish to recognize Wiccan marriage, then in the eyes of the Roman Catholic Church, Wiccan couples would not be considered married.

However, separating legal marriage from non-legal marriage results in several small problems, all of which are easily correctable. First, we can't call both the government and religious "marriage" the same thing. Since marriage implies solemnization, then marriage should be the term used in the non-legal context. For the legal context authorized by government, marriage should be replaced with the term *civil union*. That way, the two institutions remain mutual exclusive.

Second, what should the limitation of civil unions be? **None**. Now that the non-legal context of marriage is removed from the public institution, there should be no restrictions on civil unions. Since civil unions are merely personal partnerships for the purpose of legal benefits under the law, this

The Modern Paradigm of Liberty

should allow for any two or more people to form a civil union for any reason.

This would more closely emulate a *limited liability partnership* (LLP), which is a legal entity already recognized under the law. So, if several people, even relatives (such as siblings, parent-child, etc.) wish to form a civil union, they should be allowed to do so.

Keep in mind, the civil union as described above does **not** imply any existence of the non-legal attributes, such as sexual activity. So, a civil union between a parent and a child does not imply incest, but rather that the two are forming a legal partnership for mutual legal benefit.

Third, if the legal and non-legal are separate, does that mean that a religious marriage retains the same legal recognition of a civil union? **Yes**. Government could modify the authority already vested in religious leaders to continue to perform marriages in their traditional sense, with the notion that the marriage will automatically invoke the civil union in the same way that already exists.

In the end, everybody wins. Same-sex couples could have their civil unions and even be married in religious environments that accept their lifestyle, the marriage institutions of traditional religions are protected and insolated from government actions, and the people as a whole have a broader freedom with the generic civil union concept.

After all, in a society which recognizes that everyone is entitled to life, liberty and the pursuit of happiness, every means that government could take to expand one's liberties should always be explored, providing they don't infringe on the liberties of others.

Author's Supplement:

In a very real sense, the societal difference between secular and non-secular marriage is already the case. For example, government/society has the authority to certify a divorce for whatever reason the couple decides upon. But, in the eyes of the Roman Catholic Church, they are still married unless the church certifies an **annulment**. This simple and active example proves that society already recognizes and accepts the difference between the religious institution of marriage and the legal partnership of marriage.

Teamwork

Teamwork is rather celebrated in our society. In fact, it is often encouraged. From childhood sports to the corporate environment, we are continuously bombarded with the notion that "Together Everyone Achieves More." Sure, this sounds like a good idea, but is it? Moreover, is it realistic? Is it by nature for people to operate in teams or is it our nature to operate as individuals?

The notion of a team in the true meaning of the word ***teamwork*** is, in reality a farce. It is easy to celebrate a so-called team when the team succeeds, because they all can revel in the accolades. But even in success, there tends to be members of those teams who excel as well as members who under perform or are merely along for the ride. Thus, all team members are ***not*** equal, which is contrary to the team concept.

The best example of this truism is in professional sports. Despite the fact that most professional sports employ a team concept, the reality is that there are only a few star players on each team. Plus, there are also "All-Star" games and MVPs to further denote individual successes. In a true teamwork model, none of these would exist.

More importantly, what happens when the team fails? What then? Well, a true team should accept the failure equally as a whole. But in reality, there is blame-storming. "We lost the game because you missed the easy catch." "The project failed because you forgot to complete your work on time." While often times quotes like these may not be actually verbalized, they are at least thought by the so-called teammates.

What it all boils down to is this; when the chips are down, the average person goes into a CYA-mode in an effort to protect and shield themselves from the overall failure of the team.

But then, in both success and failure, we are often still reminded that we are all a team and we all share in the glory and the pain. We are all one. We each contribute a meaningful and equal part for the benefit of the whole. Therefore, we are not individuals, we are all one serving one collective greater good, even at personal sacrifice.

Perhaps this author is being cynical, but this sounds a lot like communism. Is that what we want to teach our children, our employees, and our society? If so, then repeal the Bill of Rights now and replace the field of stars on the American flag with a Hammer and Sickle. Personally, I like my individually.

So if it all the same to the rest of you, maybe there is no "I" in TEAM, but there is an "M" and an "E" and that spells ME.

President Andrew Johnson

When the average American is asked who they believe would be listed among the greatest Presidents of the United States, the common responses include names like Jefferson, Lincoln, Washington, Roosevelt and Kennedy. But there is an unsung hero of the American Presidency, one whose single and brave, yet seldom recognized achievement makes him the most underappreciated President in American history. His name is Andrew Johnson.

This very brief history of Andrew Johnson begins with his selection by Abraham Lincoln as the Vice President on the 1864 ticket. At that time, a Presidential ticket did not require that both candidates be of the same political party. So, as a token gesture to symbolize a healing and reunifying nation at the end of a Civil War, Republican Abraham Lincoln from the North selected Democrat Andrew Johnson from the South.

This brilliant strategy by President Lincoln did not sit well with the Republican Majority in Congress.

Of course, Lincoln was re-elected with Johnson as his Vice President. Upon Lincoln's assassination, Johnson ascended to the Presidency, which infuriated the Republican majority in Congress. The Republican majority attempted the closest thing to a "coupe de tat" in America for this period. They knew they could not forcibly remove the President, so they turned to their only constitutionally sound option; Impeachment. They tried and tried, digging deep into President Johnson's past to look for something they could charge him with criminally, but Johnson's history was otherwise clean.

As a last ditch effort, the Republican majority concluded that if they cannot impeach and ultimately remove Johnson, they would limit his power as President. So, since President Johnson was still operating with President Lincoln's Cabinet, Congress drafted a bill to restrict the President's power by requiring the President to first obtain Congressional approval prior to terminating anyone in the Cabinet. The first two times it passed through Congress, President Johnson of course vetoed it. But the third time's a charm, so Congress passed this into law.

President Johnson was outraged. The reason why he vetoed the bill the two previous times was because it overtly violated the separation of powers structured by the U.S. Constitution. He believed so strongly in the separation of powers and the U.S. Constitution that when this law was passed, he boldly, bravely and publicly fired his Secretary of War.

Seeing that President Johnson overtly violated new federal law, Congress jumped on the chance to impeach him. The House of Representatives did vote to impeachment Johnson, which sent the matter to the Senate. In short, after a lengthy trial, Andrew Johnson arose victorious by beating the impeachment charges, which overturned the unconstitutional law passed by Congress. Interestingly enough, Johnson won by only a single vote.

The historical significance here is very important to the framework and structure of the American government. Had Andrew Johnson not bravely challenged the dominating forces of both Houses of Congress, then the short sightedness of a group of self-serving politicians would have allowed for the gradual undermining of one of the most important preventions against tyranny in the United States.

The separation of powers conceived by the founders is specifically designed to prevent any one branch of government from having more power than the other two branches. It appears that Andrew Johnson was a truly believer in the U.S. Constitution, lived up to his oath of office, and was willing to risk everything for what he believed in. Despite his brave efforts and being a champion of the U.S. Constitution, ironically, Andrew Johnson was not re-elected.

So-Called Liberalism

Liberal. It's such a dirty word, isn't it? Or is it? The word Liberal has been so attacked by the Right and abandoned by the Left that it has lost all respect in American society. Historically, "Liberal" and "Liberalism" have been catch-all words used to describe the politics of the extreme Left in the United States. But what does *Liberal* really mean? According to the Merriam-Webster's Dictionary, the definitions of Liberal and Liberalism are as follows:

Liberal: **5** : Broad-Minded; *especially* : not bound by authoritarianism, orthodoxy, or traditional forms, **6 a** : of, favoring, or based upon the principles of liberalism **b** *capitalized*: of or constituting a political party advocating or associated with the principles of political liberalism; *especially* : of or constituting a political party in the United Kingdom associated with ideals of individual especially economic freedom, greater individual participation in government, and constitutional, political, and administrative reforms designed to secure these objectives[1] (**Note: this only includes those portions of the definition of Liberal that are relative to American politics**)

Liberalism: **1** : the quality or state of being liberal, **2 a** *often capitalized* : a movement in modern Protestantism emphasizing intellectual liberty and the spiritual and ethical content of Christianity **b** : a theory in economics emphasizing individual freedom from restraint and usually based on free competition, the self-regulating market, and the gold standard **c** : a political philosophy based on belief in progress, the essential goodness of the human race, and the autonomy of the individual and standing for the protection of political and civil liberties **d** *capitalized* : the principles and policies of a Liberal party.[2]

Looking closely at the definitions of Liberalism and Liberal, we can clearly see that Liberalism embraces "progress" and "the autonomy of the individual and standing for the protection of political and civil liberties." Clearly, Liberalism, by *definition*, allows for a society to grow and mature as it aspires towards pure freedom while respecting the rights of all individuals. Now how could any patriotic American who subscribes to the notion of a free society be opposed to that? The answer lies in the public perception of the words.

Oftentimes, the Right attempts to equate Socialism/Communism with Liberal policies. The definitions of Socialism/Communism are addressed in an earlier discussion (see Atheism vs. Socialism). Comparing the definitions of Socialism/Communism with Liberalism/Liberal plainly shows that the two philosophies are completely different and that should be plainly obvious to the casual observer.

The problem stems from the politics of Left politicians promoting many so-called liberal policies and programs in American politics. These include social programs like Welfare, Affirmative Action, Social Security, and Medicare. But are these programs truly examples of Liberalism? Clearly not. These programs represent socialism.

These programs are designed to make large sections of the population **dependent** on government and not **"autonomous"** as the definition of liberalism suggests, nor are they "associated with ideals of individual economic freedom." Further they clearly do not support "a theory in economics emphasizing individual freedom from restraint and based on free competition, the self-regulating market, and the gold standard."

In all these cases illustrated, many *so-called* liberal policies of the Left do not satisfy the actual definitions of what liberalism truly means. Obviously, there is a clear misuse and, as a result, misunderstandings of what the words Liberal and Liberalism mean in the American culture.

In truth, **true** Liberalism is great for a society that celebrates liberties and aspires towards pure freedom. But the popular understanding of Liberalism has corrupted this original meaning and since the public perception and understanding of

Sean McPhillips

Liberalism is substantially different from what the definition clearly states, it will forever remain the political scarlet letter.

---

[1] *http://www.m-w.com/cgi-bin/dictionary, search word "Liberal".*
[2] *http://www.m-w.com/cgi-bin/dictionary, search word "Liberalism".*

Celebrity

Celebrity status is the American dream for many people. With this status come fame, recognition, money and power. But why? Why does our society reward the celebrity with so much? Isn't it enough that they are famous? Must they have the wealth and power too?

When we look at Hollywood superstars, popular musicians, and professional athletes, we see that they make millions of dollars for doing what would otherwise be considered trivial work. All they really do is provide us with some level of temporary entertainment. While we all enjoy the escape from reality in being entertained, the fact is that celebrities provide little value to our society, yet are rewarded at the highest level.

First, let us examine their compensation. Why should an actor receive millions of dollars for a roll in a single movie? Sometimes, a single actor is the biggest expense in the movie. Is that necessary? Do they really add value? And what if the movie is a flop, largely do to the performance of the multi-million dollar actor? Are they accountable?

Then there is the case of professional athletes, particularly those in sports like baseball, football, and basketball. Some of these players have multi-year contracts guaranteeing tens of millions of dollars, regardless of their performance. Again, what if they under perform? Are they held accountable?

Now, this flawed model does not apply to all professional sports. Sports such as tennis and golf are truly performance based. The better the player performs, the more money they make. The less they perform, the less money they make. Ultimately, if they fail to perform for any length of time, they fall off the circuit.

So why can't this model apply to all sports. Let us take baseball for an example. All players should receive the same league minimum salary. From there, players would receive an additional unit compensation for every winning game they have played. Further, additional bonuses would be given for certain specific activities, such as home runs, no-hitters, perfect games, etc. In addition, bonuses would be given for teams to make/win the playoffs and make/win the World Series. All players would be treated equally with an equal chance to succeed. Those that perform well will maximize their compensation. Those that fail to perform, will make minimal compensation as a product of their own failure.

Better yet, why can't this model apply to all forms of entertainment? The big name Hollywood actors, who would normally command the multi-million dollar movie contracts, would instead receive a marginal minimum compensation for their efforts and then a percentage of the box office sales. If the movie fails to sell tickets, then the big name movie star (who was likely procured for the purpose of drawing audience appeal) would be minimally compensated as they have failed to live up to their value.

Second, let us examine the so-called power of celebrity. This completely escapes me. While the celebrity status gives these people recognition, it does not provide them with any special knowledge to pontificate on any subject. Oftentimes, their subjective drivel is nothing more than emotional pandering and condescending rhetoric from platitude. Just because a celebrity has recognition, does not give them any special power to speak at Congressional hearings or lecture the masses on any issue. Their opinions are no better than yours or mine, but they only get the press because they are famous.

The truth is that celebrities have this power because we give it to them. They make this money because we allow it. We, as a society need to strip celebrities of their undeserving elite status and reduce them to the contemporary equivalent of the Court Jester. They exist simply for our amusement and nothing more, and they should be treated as such.

Discrimination

Ideally, everyone should treat everyone else fairly and equally in our society. But, in reality, people have biases and preconceived notions that influence their decision-making process. That is just the way it is and there is no escaping it. Fortunately, we live in a free society where our personal opinions are not criminal.

Although the vast majority of our society opposes the public display of groups like the Neo-Nazis or the KKK, the fact is in a free society, anyone is allowed to have unpopular ideas and even express them publicly, as long as they do not infringe on the rights of other people. To criminalize such ideas would be tantamount to a "thought police".

So, if biases are allowed to exist in a free society, should the exercise of biases also be allowed? Frankly, **Yes**. If you own a car/home and you do not want someone of a particular ethnicity or belief system in/on your property, it is certainly within your right to restrict him or her. Similarly, if you wholly owned a magazine/website and a company with political views opposite yours wanted to purchase advertising space, it is well within your right to decline them advertising.

The question is; where do we draw the line? Let us take this to the next level. If you wholly owned a company or organization and someone with different beliefs and/or ethnicity wanted to be an employee or member, should you still have the right to deny that individual employment or membership? In a truly free society, unfortunately the answer is **Yes**. That is the right of the company owner; a private company should be allowed to discriminate against anybody for any reason, simply because the company is *privately* owned.

However, anyone who does discriminate limits the benefits gained from including those they discriminate against. For example, if a company discriminates against Jews in their hiring process, they would likely be discounting quality people who could benefit their business in place of non-Jews that may be of less quality.

Now, while a company policy of discrimination may be stupid and self-defeating, it should still be the right of the company owner in a free society. If a company's position is based on some unfair bias, then that is a testament to the poor quality of their character, but it is still their right. However, it is also *our* right as consumers to refuse to do business with them, boycott their products or services and expose them for their bigotry.

Now, if the company is publicly traded, then different rules apply as they are a **public** company and not private. In the case of publicly traded companies, they same rules that apply to government-sponsored services should also apply. For example, you can discriminate against someone who rides in your car, but the public transit system cannot discriminate against anyone, as they are representative of the public as a whole. Government and the law has to treat you fairly, but private citizens and private organizations do not.

Interestingly, the law very narrowly defines discrimination. Only specifically enumerated categories are protected. A company cannot fire you for being Jewish, but can fire you for being a Yankees Fan. Being a Yankees Fan is not a protected minority under discrimination laws.

In truth, the best mechanism to combat discrimination in a free society is to expose those who discriminate for what they are doing, educate the public and boycott their products and services if necessary. Ultimately, this will have a negative impact on their business and will hit them where it hurts the most, in the wallet.

When the accusation of bias is charged, particularly ethnic bias, people and organizations tend to fear this accusation and succumb to the public pressure. In a free society, it is not the role of government to sponsor politically correct thought.

Sean McPhillips

However, in a free society, it is the role of people to express themselves and their opinions, particularly when they don't like the position of others.

What Does Pro-Choice Really Mean?

Ever since Roe vs. Wade, the issue of abortion has been a political hot potato. The debate has been reduced to the polar argument of "Right to Life" vs. "Pro-Choice." While there are plenty of moral, ethical, and religious arguments to debate this subject from, it is this author's opinion that government should not base any decisions from any of these three positions simply because they have no authority to do so.

However, government does have the authority to enforce the law and invoke the will of the United States Constitution. The ruling by the Supreme Court in favor of the right for a woman to have an abortion is mostly tied to the 14th Amendment. To simplify for discussion, Section 1 of the 14th Amendment states, "All persons **born** or naturalized in the United States...are citizens of the United States" and further states that "no state shall make or enforce any law which shall abridge the privileges or immunities of citizens." This is then tied to the 4th Amendment, where it states "the right of the people to be secure in their persons...shall not be violated."

These are reasonably sound Constitutional arguments and largely the basis of the abortion ruling. At its core, the ruling is founded on this basic argument: the Constitution states that only persons born are citizens entitled to Constitutional protection and unborn human life does not meet that basic criteria, and therefore is not afforded such rights.

But when the 14th Amendment was ratified in 1868, who could have conceived the level of prenatal medicine that now exists? The U.S. Constitution is a dynamic document that is designed to grow with this county as we continue to aspire towards a purely free society where the rights of individuals are ideally protected.

As previously stated, this country is a democracy asserted as a republic, where the rights and opinions of the majority cannot trump the rights and liberties of minorities and individuals, i.e. protection from the tyranny of the majority. The question is: does this same basic argument apply to the scenario of a pregnant woman? Perhaps it does.

Without question, a developing fetus is human life. Although this human life is parasitical of a human host, that does not diminish the fact that it is still human life nonetheless. In this illustration, we have two human lives in a symbiotic relationship, one has the majority of control and the other is the minority subjected to the will of the majority.

The Modern Paradigm of Liberty

Assuming we suspend the verbatim letter of 14th Amendment and apply contemporary common sense for a moment, this situation is a classic example of tyranny of the majority, where the mother's right to choose to terminate her pregnancy supersedes the right of the fetus to live. This is not unlike conjoined twins. Can one conjoined twin terminate the life of the other to free itself of such a burden? Of course not.

So, does this argument hold Constitutional weight? In this author's opinion, it does and, surprisingly in the same area of the Constitution. While Section 1 of the 14th Amendment states "no state shall make or enforce any law which shall abridge the privileges or immunities of **citizens**," this statement continues "nor shall any State deprive any **person** of life, liberty or property, without due process of law; nor deny to any **person** within its jurisdiction the equal protection of the laws."

What is interesting here is that the 14th Amendment states that all **persons** and not just citizens within the jurisdiction of the United States are afforded equal protection under the law. This includes any person who is a non-citizen, such as resident aliens, foreigner tourists, diplomats, and perhaps unborn children. In short, there is no Constitutional disqualification of unborn children as persons.

Although the Supreme Court considered this argument, their ruling concluded two things with respect to this point: that the Constitution does not define the word **person** and that all references to a **person** in Section 1 of the 14th Amendment applies post-natally. However, with the exception of a few previous, and very recent case-law references, there is no direct identification of how or why the Supreme Court could constitutionally make such a claim.

Perhaps a better way to dissect the issue would be to segregate it into two sub-arguments. The pro-choice position is that "women have a right to choose." Choose what? Choose to terminate their pregnancy or terminate the life of the fetus? Although these two positions essentially mean the same thing today, let us fast-forward the clock 50 years or so, where prenatal medicine has advanced by substantial leaps and bounds.

In the not-to-distant future, what if prenatal medicine advanced to the point where physicians can safely remove a fetus from the human host at any point past 4 weeks of conception? Once removed, the fetus would then be inserted into an artificial maturation chamber where the fetus can continue to mature through prenatal development independent of the human host.

Here, the argument of abortion has to be completely redefined. Does a woman have the right to choose to terminate her pregnancy or terminate the life of the fetus? In this futuristic scenario, a woman can still maintain complete control over her body without sacrificing the life of the fetus.

Would the pro-choice supporters still support abortion in this case? If the fetus is removed from the human host and inserted in the artificial maturation chamber physically independent of the mother, does the woman still retain the right to terminate the life of the fetus? Better yet, if the fetus is independent of the human host, does the father now have equal rights to terminate the life of the fetus, even if the mother wants to keep it? (This argument is presented because of the current stance where a mother can terminate the fetus, even against the father will.)

Okay, the example above is pure science fiction and not for public debate today simply because it is not an option. But it does represent the likely future of this case and forces us to understand the abortion issue at its core. Obviously, all persons are protected equally under the law, not just citizens. If not, it would not be a crime to otherwise criminally victimize non-citizens. According to the 14th Amendment, non-citizens are equally protected under the law and such protection should be extended to the most defenseless and innocent of them all.

Public Breast Feeding

We have all seen it, on a train, on a bus, in a restaurant, and even at work. The question is, do we want to, or better yet, do we have to? *NO!* The basic argument for public breast feeding is this: A mother has decided to breast feed her child; the child is hungry; breast feeding is a natural act that dates back to the dawn of the species. Therefore, women should be allowed to care for their young as they need to, when they need to, wherever they need to, and in the manner they need to. But why do I have to see it?

While public breast feeding is natural and as old as mankind itself, it is still a sloppy and disgusting physical act that can be nauseating to many people, myself included. Just because breast feeding is a natural act does not mean that it is okay for public viewing. If I were in Central Park, New York City in the middle of the day, dropped my pants, propped my elbows on my knees and, with a furrowed brow, squeeze out a hideous intestinal sculpture on the lawn in full view of a public crowd, some people might consider that to be socially unacceptable. But apparently, it is okay for dogs.

Yeah, I know the argument against public defecation and urination is that there are bathrooms for that and people can "hold it in." Well, sometimes, you can't hold it in anymore! And besides, defecation and urination applies to more of the population than breast feeding does, so why would breast feeding be considered acceptable in public and defecation/urination not acceptable?

I suspect that it comes down to the hungry baby. Nobody wants to see a baby starve, but the baby could wait an extra 10-20 minutes until the mother gets to the rest room where she could do that in a private stall. The baby won't die or even be sick if it had to wait, it would just be hungry and cry. But, if you really had to take a pee, sometimes waiting the 10-20 minutes to get to a bathroom simply is not an option.

This discussion may seem intentionally graphic, if not humorous to make a point: **we are not animals**. 1000 years ago, defecating, urinating, and breast feeding in public were all common. But today in contemporary American society, we think of ourselves as more civilized than publicly reducing ourselves to our baser instincts. As leaders in the civilized world, we have a responsibility to set the example of civility.

The Healthcare Customer

For many years, the healthcare customer was always considered to be the patient. At a time when health insurance was virtually nonexistent, the majority of patients made their healthcare decisions based on what they could personally afford.

Simultaneously, healthcare during this period was reasonably simple. The costly modern medical advances that exist today simply did not exist years ago. Therefore, the cost of treatment was proportionately much cheaper in decades past.

Then, we introduced Medicare, Medicaid, and the private health insurance companies. What quickly happened was that price was removed from the equation with respect to the customer, i.e. the patient. To put it simply, a patient who has a fixed deductible on their policy would pay the same amount for healthcare services regardless of how much it *really* costs.

For example, if a patient needs a procedure and has a $500 deductible, and Dr. Smith charges $8,000 and Dr. Jones charges $12,000 for the same procedure, which doctor should the patient use? In the eyes of the patient, it doesn't matter because the cost to him is the same, $500. But in the eyes of the insurance company, there is a $4,000 difference in price.

While the above is a simple illustration, it represents the crux of the problem associated with insurance companies denying the full amount of healthcare bills. What we have is an entire market where the primary consumer is *not* price sensitive. Do you have any idea what that means?

If the price of a dozen eggs currently ranges from $1.50 to $1.75, you could shop around and get the best product for the best price. The prices are controlled by supply and demand. But, if you only have to pay $1.25 and somebody else paid the difference regardless of how much the grocer charged, would the actual price of eggs matter to you? The grocer could charge $5.00 for a dozen eggs and you would still pay only $1.25. You are no longer price sensitive. If you did have to pay the entire amount, you would *never* pay $5.00 for a dozen eggs.

This is what has been happening in the healthcare industry for the past few decades. Add to this the fact that technology and malpractice litigation have substantially influenced the cost of healthcare and the staggering rise in healthcare costs becomes blatantly evident.

The Modern Paradigm of Liberty

Healthcare insurance companies play a very valuable role in the healthcare market. They serve as the price-sensitive customer in the equation. They keep the prices of healthcare from completely sky-rocketing. What insurance companies are **NOT** doing is making medical decisions, as some people would like you to believe.

Currently, many health insurance policies have a fixed deductible for prescription medication, such as $5 regardless the actual cost of the drugs. They also often employ an 80/20 rule, where the insurance company pays 80% and the patient pays 20% for the services. In addition, there is often a cap on the patient contribution of $5,000, where the patient will not incur any costs over $5,000 regardless of the total expenses and superseding 80/20 rule.

Similar models have been imposed by insurance companies in an effort to control costs by returning some of the price sensitivity to patients. However, there is still the fixed deductible for prescription medication and a maximum patient contribution. For big ticket items and medication, the patient is still not very price sensitive. Also, the health insurance example above is just one model as there is no consistency in health insurance plans from provider to provider, making it difficult to compare apples-to-apples.

A way in which price sensitivity can be completely returned to the customer/patient is by imposing a percent-only paradigm across the board. This would mean that patients would be required to pay the same fixed percentage rate of the ***entire*** healthcare expenses regardless of their insurance carrier.

For example, patients would be required to pay 10% of all medical expenses, including operations, procedures, medication, doctor visits, and hospital stays. Insurance companies would pay the remaining 90%. So, if the patient has $80,000 is medical bills, they have to pay $8,000. There would be no cap on the patient's contribution.

Price sensitivity needs to exist in any market to keep prices under control. The most logical party to be price sensitive is the consumer, i.e. the patient. In addition, the healthcare insurance company also has a right to be price sensitive since they are paying the brunt of the expense.

Without healthcare insurance companies, the only other force capable of controlling the costs of healthcare would be government, and that would lead us down the undesirable path of socialized medicine. Given the poor quality of healthcare in nations with a socialized system, that is the last thing Americans want, particularly in a capitalist society.

Suing Health Insurance Providers

Since health insurance providers are considered part of the equation with respect to treatment, some people have suggested that they should be held accountable for their decisions. First, let us make something perfectly clear, health insurance providers do **NOT** make medical decisions, they make business decision.

A health insurance provider cannot prevent a patient from seeking treatment; they can simply choose not to pay for it. Oftentimes, the situation is not that the health insurance company refuses payment, but simply will not pay the entire bill as they have concluded the cost is too expensive. As the price sensitive customer (see previous discussion), they have that right.

This has often been interpreted as patients not being able to see *their* doctor. This is not true. A patient could see any doctor they want, but if their doctor chooses not to do business with the insurance company, or vice versa, then the patient must pay full price.

In many cases, the reason why the doctor would not accept a given insurance is because the insurance provider and the physician could not come to terms on price. To put it simply, the doctor was too expensive. Well, excuse me, but I would like to drive a Mercedes, but I can only afford a Saturn, does that mean I have a **right** to drive a Mercedes? No, it doesn't. I buy what I can afford and/or maybe the Mercedes is overpriced.

Some people even suggest that patients should have the right to file suit against their insurance companies if a claim is denied. Remember, it is the **claim** that is denied, and not the treatment. A patient could still receive treatment if their claim is denied. It just means that the patient would have to pay for the difference not covered by their insurer.

Suing an insurance company for denying the claim has no basis in medical practice. Remember, the insurance company is not making a medical decision; they are making the *business* decision. If the insurance companies weren't part of the consumer equation at all and patients had to make the purchase decision alone, patients could only pay what they could afford and would even be in a position to negotiate the price with the healthcare providers. That is what insurance companies do now.

What those who support suing insurance companies fail to realize is that by allowing suits to exist, insurance companies would have to raise their rates and ultimately the cost of healthcare would go up. Further, health insurance would likely be available to fewer people as insurance companies would scale back their service offerings to individuals and businesses in an effort to mitigate the risk of suit.

That means people could lose their medical benefits even if they are employed. Employers do not have a legal obligation to provide people with medical benefits, and even if they did, the increase cost of insurance would be offset by a reduction in employee salary.

There is an alternative to suit for denied claims. If a patient's claim is denied but chooses to have the treatment anyway, fronts the costs of the treatment, and the treatment is successful, then the patient should be reimbursed. The reimbursement should only be in the amount that the insurance company would normally provide for such treatment (i.e. if the patient gets treatment that costs $3,000, but the insurance company only pays $2,000, then the patient will only receive $2,000 back).

However, if the *elected* treatment is unsuccessful, then the patient must absorb the full cost of the treatment. This is because the insurance company denied the claim due to their experience in the industry. If the patient wishes to take the risks and loses against the odds of the risk, why should the insurance company incur the cost?

In any case, suing insurance companies is a bad idea, period. It just gives people another reason to blame others for their problems and sue them for it. But apparently, that appears to be the trend of the new American dream in the land of opportunity.

Before, the American dream meant if you work hard enough, you can achieve anything. Now, the opportunity is *"who we can sue for a million bucks."* Frivolous malpractice suits have existed in the medical profession for some time now. Since people know that insurance companies have deep pockets, it is only natural that they are next.

Priests and Pedophilia

Public attention has recently been brought to bear on a problem that has plagued the Catholic Church for an untold number of years. The issue is as shocking as it is heinous. These men of the cloth who profess to be men of God, who lecture their flock on morals and ethical standards, who are the absolvers of *our* sins, have overtly violated the sacred trust of their most vulnerable parishioners. But if that isn't bad enough, what is worse is the insane debate that followed when the charges were brought forward and subjected to public scrutiny.

The defenders of these pedophiles argue that this is an internal matter of the church. Well, we can see how the church handles such matters; they reassign the priest to a new church without warning the new parish of this person's history and then sweep the whole thing under the carpet.

Sounds more like evading the truth, lying to the people and perpetuating criminal behavior and sin. Ironically, this is the same church that insists its followers regularly confess their sins and assume accountability for their actions. If they are to truly be moral leaders of society then they should set the example by which others should follow.

But what concerns this author the most is the otherwise total lack of enforcement from the secular authority for so long. Had the pedophiles been school teachers or a soccer coaches, they would have hauled them away in handcuffs a long time ago. For some reason, the clergy have been held to a higher standard of protection under the law. Excuse me for stating the obvious, but isn't everyone supposed to be treated equally under the law regardless of gender, ethnicity or religion?

What we have here is quite simple: American citizens are breaking American laws on American soil and victimizing other American citizens. Am I missing something? These priests who have abused their power and trust of their followers deserve no better treatment than any other criminal.

Finally, accountability should not end with the perpetrator. The fact is, the church new that such behavior has been a problem with priest for quite some time. But instead of reporting the criminal behavior, they shuffled these monsters onto unsuspecting new victims. This has been an ongoing activity within the church, which constitutes a conspiracy. As far as this author is concerned, the church must also bear some accountability on this issue as well, both criminally and punitively.

The Modern Paradigm of Liberty

Furthermore, the fact that the church continued to hide this activity for years further supports the conspiracy theory. Since the conspiracy began with the initial victimizations, followed by the subsequent cover-up by church officials allowing the conspiracy to exist up to and including the present, then the conspiracy links the initial crimes to the present, therefore bridging the time gap that would have been otherwise expired due to the statute of limitations.

So, those priests who molested children 20-30 years ago should still be prosecuted as if the crimes happened yesterday. Only with swift action by secular authority could justice truly be served and the innocent be protected.

Meagan's Law

How can anyone oppose Meagan's Law? This law is designed to warn the public of the presence of adults in their community that are convicted sexual predators. Any reasonable and responsible parent would want to know about any potential threat and danger to their children, especially in their own neighborhood. So, what's the problem?

Civil liberties groups argue that such a law violates the privacy of the convicted sexual predator. They further argue that these people have paid their debt to society and should not be branded with a scarlet letter.

But, what they seem to forget is that the U.S. Constitution allows for the liberties of any citizen to be temporarily or permanently restricted as a matter of due process, especially when they violate the rights of other people. Therefore, if they are convicted of a sexual crime, then the people have the authority to limit the liberties of these criminals. Besides, Meagan's Law serves as an additional deterrent to crime.

But, even if we accept this position, is there still a reason to oppose Meagan's Law? In this author's opinion, the answer is **Yes**. Here is the issue. Meagan's Law is a textbook example of mob rule creating a generic law induced from a specific case. This is not the best way to make generic policy, as it does not examine the big picture.

So, what is the big picture? Well, the Meagan's Law argument is based on this principle: If you have a child and there is a convicted sexual predator living in the neighborhood, you want to know this so that you can protect your child. This seems reasonable. But ask yourself this, if your neighbor was a convicted drug dealer, armed burglar or murderer, wouldn't you want to know that too? Meagan's Law does not require that these people register themselves with local authority.

The basic, generic, big picture approach should be this: All criminal history of any persons convicted of a felony should be available for public record, regardless of the crime. The rights of the criminal can be constitutionally restricted since the conviction is a matter of due process.

Further, the interests of the people are served so that they can take appropriate action to protect themselves and their families from potential harm in their neighborhood. In addition, the people have a basic right to know this information, as these crimes are committed against *The People*.

Finally, Meagan's Law is a good idea, but it should be fairly and evenly applied to all criminals or none at all. Personally, this author prefers the former to that latter for the reasons stated above. In addition, the generic form of Meagan's Law would also serve as an additional deterrent to crime as the criminals would suffer endless humility, as their criminal record would be on public display forever. This further asserts the accountability of these criminal acts squarely on the shoulders of the perpetrators. Call this author old fashioned, but I don't feel sorry for people who intentionally victimize others.

Eroding Freedoms

Yes, as Americans, we enjoy the freest society in history. The founding fathers conceived ideal liberty and freedom and practiced practical liberty and freedom for the period. As we matured as a nation, we continued to aspire towards the ideal model with social and governmental advances such as the abolishment of slavery and women's liberation. But some people, such as this author, would question whether many actions of government are gradually eroding the freedoms of Americans.

Throughout this book, there are many examples where government appears to be taking steps backwards in the area of American freedoms. Some of these are significant enough to be illustrated in separate discussions. However, there are other examples that we see and accept every day that have been compromising our freedoms, even if such actions are for our own protection or for the *greater good*. Let us examine a few examples:

Seat Belts: We all know that seat belts in cars will, in fact, save lives when worn properly. Statistical evidence has proven that. From personal experience, this author has been in two serious car accidents and in both cases seat belts saved my life. The evidence is so overwhelming in support of seat belts that anyone who does not wear one either has their head in the sand or is a complete idiot. But does that give the government the authority to make it a crime not to wear one?

Seat belt laws have been promoted by the insurance industry. The belief is that if more people wear seat belts, there will be fewer numbers of serious injuries in car accidents. Fewer injuries mean smaller insurance settlements. This is statistically true and a pretty solid argument in support of mandatory seat belt laws. But isn't it my car? Shouldn't I still have a choice about wearing a seat belt?

While the basic position of the insurance industry is strong, it does not validate the government to infringe on the rights of people by mandating seat belts. People have a right to choose (or not choose) to do things that could endanger their lives. Hence, this explains the existence of extreme sports. But the concern of the insurance industry is valid, that more people would be more seriously injured and, as a result, file greater pain and suffering claims. This is because we have quickly evolved into a litigious society.

The Modern Paradigm of Liberty

The solution that satisfies all angles of this problem is simple: repeal the existing seat belt law mandates. Then, pass new legislation that would put the onus on drivers and passengers. If a person is in a car accident and suffers extensive injuries because they chose not to wear their seat belt, then that person assumes full accountability for their actions.

This means they would forfeit any right to file tort suit for pain and suffering against any other party in the accident resulting in either their own insurance to cover their medical expense or be personally liable. That way, people are held accountable for their own actions and choices, frivolous litigation is curtailed, all while maintaining a little more freedom.

Cell Phones: New York was the first state to pass a law making it illegal to drive while on a hand-held cell phone. Hands-free cell phones are still legal. This law is ridiculous for two reasons. First, it is not the action of holding a cell phone that is the distraction to drivers, as many drivers drive with one hand anyway.

The distraction is the conversation on the phone itself. It is very easy to be completely distracted and immersed into a phone conversation. Haven't you ever walked up to somebody on the phone and have had to wave your hand in front of their face just to get their attention? Now, imagine that same person behind the wheel. It would make more sense if all cell phone activity was banned while driving. But, there is another problem with that.

Like with seat belts, people *choose* to speak on the phone while driving. It is their car and they can do what they want. As long as they are not infringing on the rights of anyone else, they should be allowed to do what they want. The problem occurs when they cause an accident as a result of talking on a cell phone. Well, since the driver *chose* to speak on the phone while driving, then the driver should incur a greater amount of liability associated with that accident then if the driver had not been on the phone. Accountability should fall squarely on the shoulders of the individual.

Therefore, the same approach suggested for seat belts should apply. Repeal cell phone restrictions. Then, pass new legislation that would put the onus on drivers. If a person using their cell phone causes an accident, then that person assumes full accountability for their actions.

This means they would incur a greater percentage of the liability for the accident, as well as forfeit their right to file tort suit for pain and suffering against any other party in the accident and result in either their own insurance to cover their medical expense or be personally liable. Again, people are held accountable for their own actions and freedoms remain intact.

Coral Springs, Florida: This is a small city in south Florida, just north of Ft. Lauderdale. Coral Springs is very clean, aesthetically pleasing, has good schools, low crime and is an all-around nice place to live, as long as you cooperate. Coral Springs has a city-wide ordinance that limits the presentation of personal property. Specifically, Coral Springs has a specific palette of colors that all private homes must conform to.

According to the law in Coral Springs, if a home owner decided to paint his home, he would have to obtain a no-fee permit from the Community Development Department of the City of Coral Springs. To receive an approved permit, the home owner must submit paint samples of the desired colors with the application for the permit. This law applies to primary, secondary and trim colors.

Coral Springs contends that there is a wide variety of approved colors, but this implies in the language that all colors must be approved by the city. To put it simply, it is literally against the law to paint your home a color outside of the city approved and controlled palette of colors.

Again, good intentions probably invoked this law. This was probably imposed to keep the décor of the neighborhoods consistent, as well as protect the value of some of the neighborhoods from those who would willfully present their house in a manner that is otherwise atypical and not flattering to the surrounding homes. But isn't that a risk of living in any neighborhood? What gives the city of Coral Springs the authority to assert that a resident cannot paint their house any color they want?

Sean McPhillips

****

The problem with all three of these examples is that violations of these laws are only punishable by a minimal fine. The fine is enough of an annoyance to deter people from breaking these laws but is not a substantial punishment to invoke anyone to challenge the constitutionality of these laws. Thus, these minor infringements on our personal freedoms are allowed to exist on the books and go unchallenged.

This is very troublesome as is allows American citizens to become acclimated and ultimately complacent towards the existence of such restrictions on our freedoms. Once we become used to these limitations of our freedom as the norm, more infringements will soon follow.

Eventually, we will wake one day and look back on the decades of these gradual steps that eroded our free expression in an effort to assimilate all Americans into a unified culture controlled by the tyranny of the majority. Many New Yorkers are beginning to realize this now that smoking is banned from all public bars and restaurants in New York City.

What we can do today is simply not accept these minor infringements on our liberties. We need to contact our politicians at all levels, hold public meeting, write editorials, and simply stand up and say "*No*". Without taking these actions today, we will watch our freedoms continue to erode in the years to come. Given that we have the opportunity to intercede now, we would have only ourselves to blame should the erosion of American freedoms continue.

Airport Security and the Fourth Amendment

Since September 11th, 2001, the public cried out for a more secure screening process at the airports. This is propagated by the fact that the 9/11 terrorist managed to slip box cutters through the security checkpoint and used these implements as instruments of terrorism. So, it stands to reason that security measures need to be stricter to maximize the security of air travel. But at what price?

Benjamin Franklin once said "*Those who would trade liberty for security deserves neither liberty nor security.*" In the post-9/11 scare, many people were willing to allow for any level of airport security to exist just for the illusion of feeling safe, even if it did not provide any real security.

Temporary security measures included posting national guardsman at the security checkpoints, more thorough searches of passengers and their belongings, and the random searches of passengers at the gate. While it is somewhat understandable for people in fear to allow for these so-called heightened security measures to exist in the short-term, the fact remains that they are still violations of our liberties and we as Americans should not stand for it.

So what is too far? On April 2nd, 2002, airport security at John F. Kennedy International Airport forced 40 year old Elizabeth McGarry to drink from three separate bottles of her own breast milk to insure that the liquid did not pose a threat to other passengers. The good news for all Americans is that Ms. McGarry ultimately stood up to Airport Security at this ridiculous infringement on her personal freedom, which lead to the repeal of this mandate by the Transportation Security Administration (TSA). Ms. McGarry is a great American example for all of us to follow.

But is there more? Yes. Having national guardsmen at the security checkpoint is also unacceptable. If you are going through security and the security guard clearly goes to far as in the case of Ms. McGarry, what do you do? Do you complain and make an issue out of the situation? Would you be willing to make a scene defending your rights knowing that there is a soldier with an automatic weapon ten feet away?

Actor/Comedian Kevin Meany found out the hard way when he was traveling with his wife and toddler. Some confusion arose and Mr. Meany's child started running off. When he attempted to retrieve his child, he was forcibly detained by the National Guard. Like any other parent would in that circumstance, he shoved the guardsman aside and managed to get free to retrieve his two-year old. Of course, Mr. Meany was arrested and detain for several hours. All charges were later dropped. This raises the question of the value of posting the National Guard at the airport. Really, how many planes in history were ever high-jacked at the security checkpoint?

Of all these gross infringements on our rights and liberties, the biggest has to be the random checking of passengers and baggage. First of all, random checking does NOT check all passengers. Casual observation of random searches will reveal their search pattern, which when identified, can be used to avoid the random search. This completely defeats the purpose of the random search.

Additionally, now the TSA has the authority to not only randomly search your checked baggage, but to do so without your presence or prior knowledge. This means that they can open and search through random bags as they see fit. Of course when they do so, they kindly remind you that they violated your rights with a little **Notification of Baggage Inspection** that they put inside your luggage, which includes a reference to *Section 110(b) of the Aviation and Transportation Security Act of 2001* to justify their violation of your rights. Even worse, if your baggage is locked to secure your belongings from theft, the TSA will cut the lock without your permission and without compensation.

Further, what gives the TSA constitutional authority to randomly search otherwise law-abiding citizens? If a police officer were to stop people at random on the street and ask them to empty out their pockets, purses, briefcases, etc, would that be acceptable? **Absolutely not.** So, why is it acceptable in the airport?

This is just another clear example of the security going just too far. If you disapprove of the way security is being handled, do you have a choice to protest? If you think you do, you are wrong. Try it and see what happens. First, you will not make your flight, period. Second, you will almost certainly be detained. Interestingly enough, the security will **ask** you if they can randomly search your bag. They ask you to be polite, but do you really have a choice? Again, try politely declining their request and see what happens.

Now, this author is not unreasonable. I understand that air travel is a unique commutation. While armed pilots, sky marshals, and law-abiding citizens with concealed carry licenses will help make air travel more secure, that is not the subject of this discussion. What is the subject are the violations of the 4th Amendment that have gone on since September 11th, 2001 and enough is enough.

The 4th Amendment to the United States Constitution is clear in its language, that the people have a right to be "*secure in their persons, houses, papers, and effects, against unreasonable searches and seizures*" and that "*no warrants shall issue, but upon probable cause."* This has been a long standing practice of any and all law enforcement agencies at all levels of government. Furthermore, any evidence that would be acquired during a search that was later determined to be a violation of the 4th Amendment would be deemed inadmissible in court because of the violation of the citizen's rights.

Airport security should only have the authority to require a search of someone's person or belongings with sufficient probable cause. Probable cause would likely be satisfied if the passenger trips the metal detector alarm at the security checkpoint or if the passenger's bag shows something suspicious in the x-ray.

Fortunately (or unfortunately), enforcement of any new regulation should be immediately applied since all airport security has fallen under Federal Authority via the Transportation Security Administration. The creation of the TSA is the first constitutionally correct action of government since September 11th, 2001 as it relates to airport security.

However, the TSA is still an administrative agency with their own self-defined powers, which presents its own set of Constitutional problems. The U.S. Constitution empowers the federal government to regulate any interstate activity, and air travel is no exception. Now, let's see if the federal government is willing to support the 4th Amendment as well.

In any case, the passenger should have the right to challenge any search on the spot, insist that the search be

Sean McPhillips

done in private and out of public view, and demand to see a supervisor immediately, all without fear of being treated like a criminal. After all, if they want to search your personal belongings, you still have a right to maintain your dignity.

Desecration of the American Flag

Many legislators on both sides of the Congressional isle have been entertaining the notion of a Constitutional amendment that would protect the American flag from wanton desecration. As a patriot, there seems to be little debate: if you love this country and everything it stands for, then any symbol that represents American principles should be protected from disrespect. But is the argument really that simple?

It is this author's opinion that desecration of the American flag, or any symbol of national pride is disrespectful, inappropriate and unacceptable. But that is just one man's opinion. However, there are those who believe that political statements can be emphasized by using an American flag as an instrument of controversy. In a truly free society, they should be allowed to do so, regardless of the opinions of others.

Remember that the fundamental principle of a republic is to celebrate the rights of individuals, providing that the expression of those liberties do not violate the rights of others. Most criminal laws in the American legal system are specifically design to criminalize behavior that victimizes other citizens. Since desecration of an American flag does not infringe or violate anyone's liberties or rights, then there is no need to criminalize this act, as there is no victim.

Further, the mission of the Constitution is clear within its content. In short, the mission of Constitution is to define the structure and powers of government as well as enumerate the rights of people, as discussed earlier. A Constitutional amendment that is specifically designed to protect the American flag is counteractive to this mission, as it would be specifically designed to narrow a form of expression that is otherwise free.

In a society that is the benchmark of international freedom, it would be ironic that we would go out of our way to specifically restrict expression in any form. Even if actual occurrences of public desecration of the American flag are few and far between, it is still a right that people should be allowed to express.

While the founders recognized the American flag would symbolize freedom, they probably never conceived the notion that a patriot would ever exercise such disrespect. James Madison, author of the 1st Amendment, which protects freedom of expression, has been known to personally oppose the desecration of the American flag.

Interestingly enough, the founders did not see it fit to specifically restrict desecration of the American flag. Could this be because they fully understood what the mission the Constitution truly is? Or, is it because they believed that people are free to do what they want, providing they do not infringe on the rights of others?

Since the birth of this nation and the creation of the U.S. Constitution, the rights, liberties and freedoms that have been enjoyed by American citizens over the years have continued to expand the definition of a free society. It would be shameful and an insult to founders to take a monumental step backwards.

Finally, if the founders in their wisdom did not constitutionally protect the flag from desecration, then what makes it such a good idea now? Further, for those who are willing to support the intentional narrowing of any liberties within the United States via constitutional language, this author questions their commitment to a free society. This is because free speech does not protect the speech that you like; it protects the speech that you hate. If free speech only protected the speech that you like, then it isn't free speech.

The Pledge of Allegiance

Recent judicial rulings, as well as political and public debate have raised issue on the constitutionality of the Pledge of Allegiance. This issue in question surrounds the two words "under God" and challenges the notion of church/state separation. While the vast majority of Americans may **believe** in God, a majority belief in something does not make it fact.

For example, when the majority of people believed the Earth was flat, that did not change the fact that the Earth is actually round. Belief in God is based entirely on faith, and for government to sponsor a message rooted in religious faith violates the separation of church and state.

But let us set that aside and first examine a brief history of the Pledge of Allegiance. The pledge is not as old as many people think. In fact, it was written in 1892, 116 years after the Declaration of Independence, and long after all the founding fathers died.

Sean McPhillips

In Bill O'Reilly's latest book "**Who's Looking Out For You?**", he poses this rhetorical question: "*I wonder what Jefferson would think of the ruling by the Ninth Circuit Court of Appeals in California that the word God is unconstitutional in the Pledge of Allegiance*" [1]. Well, Jefferson's response would almost certainly be: "*What is the Pledge of Allegiance?*" because Jefferson died 66 years before the Pledge was written!

That aside, prior to the introduction of the words "under God" in 1954, the constitutionality of the Pledge was surprisingly first raised by Christians, specifically Jehovah's Witnesses. Their argument was that they consider the flag to be a graven image and forcing them to affirm a Pledge violates their interpretation of the Ten Commandments. On June 3, 1940, the Supreme Court originally ruled **against** the Jehovah's Witnesses, which sparked a nationwide animosity towards Jehovah's Witnesses.[2]

The national hatred towards Jehovah's Witnesses manifested itself in acts of vandalism including burning a church in Kennebunk, Maine and acts of personal terrorism targeting Jehovah's Witnesses directly including the rounding up Jehovah's Witnesses by the police chief in Richwood, WV, placing them in the center of a mass Pledge of Allegiance recital, force-feeding them large quantities of castor oil and marching them out of town.[2]

The founding fathers would have been appalled by these actions of so-called patriotic Americans as the founders asserted religious freedom in the First Amendment to allow **anyone** to freely practice their faith without fear of prosecution or persecution. Religious persecution is why many of the early settlers fled to the New World, so they can practice *their* faiths freely.

Following these act of domestic terrorism and after hundreds of Jehovah's Witness children were expelled from school, the Supreme Court revisited their decision and reversed themselves in 1943. The Supreme Court then ruled that school children could not be forced to recite the Pledge of Allegiance, citing that *"no official, high or petty, can prescribe what shall be orthodox in politics, nationalism, religion, or other matter of opinion or force citizens to confess by word or act their faith theirin."*[2]

Despite the ruling in 1943, "under God" was added in 1954. Thus, this is not exactly a long standing American tradition. Further, adding the words "under God" in 1954 is no coincidence.

At that time, Soviet Communism was rearing its ugly head. Since formal communism adopted Atheism as their official position on religion and since the United States defined itself as the enemy and opposite of communism, adding "under God" to the Pledge of Allegiance was a deliberate act of the Eisenhower administration to link God and American government as a means to distinguish this nation from communism. Keep in mind; this was during the height of

McCarthy-ism, which was the mid-twentieth century's equivalent of a Salem witch-hunt.

But let us set the religious argument aside for the remainder of the discussion. Let us assume that the "under God" phrase was not an issue at all. Is there still any potential constitutional violation with respect to the Pledge of Allegiance, with or without "under God"? Perhaps there is.

What concerns this author more generically is that while Congress and the vast majority of people who believe that public recitation of the Pledge is patriotic (which it is), they fail to realize that if a patriotic person disagrees with part or all of the Pledge and opts not to say it, he/she can be (and often is) construed by others as being unpatriotic, which may not be the case at all. However, someone who believes in the Pledge of Allegiance in its entirety and recites it with sincerity is clearly patriotic, and they should not be deprived that freedom of expression.

But imagine yourself a 10 year old child in a classroom where the teacher and every other student rises to recite the Pledge of Allegiance. There is an enormous amount of peer pressure under those circumstances, not to mention the potential for ridicule from fellow classmates. Sure, people may not say anything to you directly (or maybe they will), but the notion that you would not stand for the Pledge of Allegiance implies a lack of patriotism.

Here is the real problem with the Pledge of Allegiance. By government sponsoring an "official" Pledge of Allegiance, they collectively imply that a patriotic person **should** say and/or believe in its content (although this is not a mandate). Does government have the Constitutional right or authority to define the benchmark of a citizen's patriotism? The answer is plainly **No**.

The concern here is that the government is suggesting what we should or shouldn't **think** which is enforced by the peer pressure of the overwhelming majority acting as an informal thought-police. The complexity in this case is that this particular "thought" is substantially grayed by patriotism and personal faith.

Furthermore, it simply does not matter in the United States that an overwhelming majority supports the Pledge as we live in a **Republic** and not a pure Democracy. Perhaps defenders of the Pledge of Allegiance should actually read the words of the Pledge. They would find that the Pledge states "*and to the* **Republic** *for which it stands*", not "to the Democracy".

For those who believe that the Pledge should remain with or without "under God" simply because a **majority** of people support it, clearly do not understand the language in the Pledge. It is painfully obvious that blind recitation of the Pledge of Allegiance does not equate to an understanding of its content.

This author gets concerned when government takes otherwise marginal actions that initially have good intentions, but in reality gradually impede on our liberties. Sure, in the case of the Pledge, very few will argue. But the official sponsoring of thought by government sets a bad precedent. The use of precedent to broadly construe the content and application of court rulings and laws in an effort to make them more applicable in broader areas of society is a common practice of attorneys and lawmakers alike.

That being said, it is not unreasonable for government to **suggest** other things we *should* be thinking and saying. Little by little, these small steps add up to big ones. Then, one day, they are all around us and we are blinded by acclimation and complacency that we do not even realize our liberties and freedoms are being violated.

Though, some may suggest that ongoing government sponsored **correct** thought will never happen. Since that would be a gross infringement on our liberties, people would publicly protest. But gradual steps that seem trivial will allow the big changes to creep in as a collection of small ones over time. If you throw a frog in a pot of boiling hot water, it will jump out. But, if you put a frog in a pot of warm water and gradually heat it up, you will eventually boil it to death.

Challenging when government marginally impedes on liberties and freedoms is never a bad thing, even if the challenge is unpopular. If people do not let the majority and/or government get away with the little steps that infringe on liberties and freedoms of minorities and individuals, then government and/or the tyranny of the majority can never get away with the big steps and freedoms and liberties will remain intact.

---

[1] O'Reilly, Bill (2003 September) "**Who's Looking Out For You?**" p.114.
[2] Johnson, Ellen (2002 July) "**From The President**" American Atheist Newsletter, Volume 41, Number 6, p1-p5 (paragraphs footnoted are paraphrased, and not verbatim).

Sexual Freedom

As previously stated numerous times in earlier essays, a free society for all citizens is built on the principle that everyone is equally entitled to life, liberty and the pursuit of happiness. This notion works and survives to this day because it applies to **everyone**, implying that the exercise of individual rights cannot infringe on the rights of others. Without question, this principle extends to the area of sexual freedom.

Prior to the 1960s, there was an unofficial culture surrounding sexual behavior, suggesting that some behavior was wrong, immoral, or even taboo. But the free love concept of the 1960s publicly challenged this notion. Today, there are people very publicly discussing their sexual practices, orientations, and behaviors.

Is that a bad thing? Well, that depends. There are those people who choose not to hear the sexual practices of others. To them, they can simply look the other way. But freedom includes being free in every context, and sexual freedom is no exception. In reality, it is probably the ultimate freedom.

Traditional sexual behavior is seldom frowned upon. Sex is obviously a necessity of procreation so all belief systems must allow for some sex to occur. But culture, often tied to religion, has turned sex into this dirty, shameful practice that should not be enjoyed as a recreational activity but only as a biological necessity, and only when married. While we in a free society need to respect the beliefs of others, this is not the choice of all.

Any sexual behavior and activity between consenting adults should be acceptable behavior in a free society, whether or not other individuals have a personal opposition to it. In a free society, people have the right to pursue happiness as they see fit, providing they do not infringe on the rights and liberties of others. Therefore, in a free society, people should be allowed to engage in any sexual activity they choose, particularly in privacy.

Senator Santorum of Pennsylvania argued against legalized sodomy by equating it to the adult incest, polygamy and adultery. Many members in the gay community were offended. I say, **so what**? In all three of these other so-called immoral behaviors suggested by the Senator, he failed to recognize the simple facts that in all of these scenarios, the adults willfully engage in consenting behavior and their actions do not infringe on the liberties of anyone else.

What gives a "free society" the authority to demonize, if not criminalize this behavior? Anyone who would force their subjective and archaic moral code on society as a whole is in direct violation to the basic concept of liberty and freedom enumerated in the U.S. Declaration of Independence and the foundation of the American way of life. In short, anyone with an IQ higher than an apple cannot simultaneously subscribe to Senator Santorum's position and believe in a free society.

However, there are those who insist that some behavior is somehow immoral, unethical, deviant, etc. These sexual practices include homosexuality, group sex, sadomasochism, bondage & discipline, and plain old kinky sex. Everybody is entitled to their opinion. But for those who voluntarily engage in these activities of their own free will and do not infringe on the liberties of anyone else, more power to them. They dare challenge popular culture in an attempt to remove these archaic man-made stigmas.

The fact is all *unorthodox* sexual behavior is not new. Traces of these behaviors date back as far as sex itself in all societies, it was just very covert. Today, we are fortunate to live in a world where we have instant access to information, as well as people willing to challenge *traditional* social doctrine for the chance to be sexually free.

Freedom begins with one's self. If people cannot be free with whom they are in their own homes and are forced to live with persecution and discrimination, then how can we convince ourselves and others that we represent the model of a free society?

Slavery Reparations

Recent debate sparked by select groups within the African-American community suggests that the current American government, businesses, organizations, and/or people should be compelled to pay reparations for the slavery of their ancestors over 140 years ago. According to the Merriam-Webster dictionary, **reparations** refer to the act of making amends, offering expiation, or giving satisfaction for a wrong or injury.

To put it simply, reparations are an effort to make right for a past wrong by the offending party. Without question, the enslaving of any group of people for any reason, especially against their will is considered to be a "wrong" or "injury" against that person, which on its face justifies the reparation. That would be all fine and good if the entire subject ended there. But it doesn't.

The fact is, the colonial Europeans who acquired the slaves from Africa did so from other Africans, i.e. they were purchased from other black men. While that does not justify the European colonials to enslave them, it does suggest that those in slavery would have been in slavery either in Africa or the United States.

The Emancipation Proclamation from the Lincoln Administration was the official act of the United States Government that freed the slaves within the domestic borders of the United States. Slavery still existed in Africa and, in some cases, still exists there today.

Upon freedom, the slaves instantly became United States citizens, entitled to all the rights of said citizenry. While ideal in theory, the practice resulted in overt discrimination and persecution requiring another century to pass before Civil Rights were asserted.

Today, in the midst of the so-called racial tension, the fact is anyone, regardless of ethnicity can succeed at anything they set their mind to. Proof is evident with the success of immigrants who migrate to the United States with limited command of the English language and manage to acquire employment, support their family and ultimately succeed in their own right.

The United States truly is the land of opportunity. True, opportunity is not equal for everyone, the wealthy and powerful have a much easier time succeeding than the underprivileged, but that is the detriment of a free society based on capitalism.

The Modern Paradigm of Liberty

Free people aren't equal, equal people aren't free (anonymous quote).

To suggest reparations for slaves immediately upon the signing the Emancipation Proclamation would have been prudent and appropriate. This is because those individuals who have been "wronged" can receive their indemnity. But to suggest that the African-Americans of today are entitled to the compensation of their ethnicity 140 years ago when they themselves have not endured the slavery hardship simply bares no continuity of logic. But, perhaps a middle ground is still viable.

Since individual reparations simply cannot be pragmatically calculated, a reparations settlement can only be issued as a class-action judgment for the entire African-American community. The most accurate way to calculate such judgment would be to estimate the value of reparations at the time of the Emancipation Proclamation and then forecast the amount to present value. That would and should be the **gross reparations indemnity**. The **gross individual indemnity** would be calculated by dividing the gross reparations indemnity by the African-American population within the United States.

But that is not the **net reparations indemnity**. In order to truly "right" a past "wrong", it should be undone to the fullest extent possible, not just compensated. That means, quite bluntly, sending them back to Africa. But it does not end there. To completely undo the "wrongs" of slavery, those deported would have to renounce their United States citizenship and all the benefits thereof retroactively.

That means, all government entitlements received by the African-American community since the Emancipation Proclamation would not have been entitled to any non-citizens. Therefore, those entitlements (such as Welfare) received by the African-American community would have to be repaid to the Federal, State and Local governments.

To account for the repayment of entitlements, the total amount of dollars paid in the form of entitlements to the African-American community would have to be estimated and also calculated into present value dollars. This would be the **entitlement repayment factor**. Once this value is calculated, then the **net reparations indemnity** would equal the gross reparations indemnity minus the entitlement repayment factor. Finally, The **net individual indemnity** would be calculated by dividing the net reparations indemnity by the African-American population within the United States.

So, for African-Americans to truly and completely receive reparations for slavery they would have to renounce their citizenship and all rights and benefits thereof, relocate to the African nation of their choice (most likely Liberia) with the assistance of the United States State Department, and be considered a foreigner like any other non-U.S. citizen.

But let's be pragmatic, this is never going to happen. What is practical is the fact that the African-Americans of today have actually already received the reparations for the slavery of their ancestors. That reparation is in the form of a birth-right United States citizenship. That may sound corny, but tell that to the countless thousands of immigrants who risk their lives and fortunes just for the chance to live in this country even if only illegally.

The value of a United States citizenship is priceless and their opportunities are endless. The fact is, had the ancestors of today's African-Americans not endured slavery; today's African-Americans would have never realized the benefits of American citizenship. After all, would they really have been better off in Rwanda, Zaire or the Sudan? Besides, the African-American community as a whole has made a significant contribution to American history and their absence would be a detriment to our society.

The Arrogance of Man

Recorded history goes back many thousands of years. Throughout history and the numerous civilizations of man, mankind has asserted his presence on the face of the Earth with creation, destruction, war, peace, conquest and achievement, all in spite of his many flaws.

Historically, the sheer arrogance of man has been a significant driving force in many of man's actions throughout the years. Much of this arrogance is in the pursuit of knowledge and science (such at the atomic bomb) while much arrogance is also rooted in the ignorance of man.

Contemporary man is no exception to arrogance. In fact, he is ripe with it. While the contemporary arrogant efforts of man could likely fill a library, the most logical illustration of his arrogance can be summed up rather succinctly.

Popular belief systems subscribe to very basic arrogant positions, and as such have made very arrogant statements.

This discussion summarizes what this author believes to be the three most arrogant statements in the history of mankind.

Number 3: "With all of our modern advances and industrialization, we are destroying the environment and the Earth".

The Earth has been around for 4.6 billion years. This planet has taken more punishment and abuse by nature than mankind could ever throw at it, especially in a passive manner like pollution. There have been countless species that have come and gone over the course of this planet's history, yet amazingly life and this planet managed to ultimately survive. These natural catastrophes include floods, earthquakes, disease, hunger, ice ages and even celestial impacts, one of which wiped out the dinosaurs.

All of these natural plagues have befallen the Earth completely independent of human existence. Now, suggesting that using an aerosol deodorant is going to somehow cause an environmental nightmare in 100 years is not only absolute nonsense it is blatantly arrogant.

Even if mankind united and made it the primary mission of our species to destroy the Earth and the environment, it is still very unlikely. But to suggest that the environment and the Earth will be destroyed simply as a byproduct of progress is absurd.

Now, this is not to condone pollution nor does this suggest that a wanton disregard for the environment and the Earth is acceptable. Not at all. The fact is we have to live here. You don't pee in your living room, do you? You have a bathroom for that. Well, it is nice to keep our planet as livable and habitable as possible.

As long as reasonable and practical measures and solutions for waste management are employed, the environment and the planet are going to be just fine. But, alas, like everything else that came before us, when the Earth is through with us, it will shake us like a bad case of fleas and make room for something else.

Number 2: "Earth contains the only life in the universe and mankind is the only (or most) intelligent life, i.e. there is no such thing as U.F.O.s and little green men"

The universe represents the epitome of what infinity is. There are countless billions of stars within our galaxy alone and countless billions of galaxies in the universe. In fact, most of the universe cannot be seen with the naked eye. Only with employed advanced astronomy instrumentation, such as the Hubble Space Telescope can we even see some of the far reaches of the universe.

Given that life evolved on this planet naturally, it stands to reason that life could likely evolve elsewhere, especially if that place has water. With the recent discoveries of the so-called fossilized microbes on a Martian rock, this raises all new questions and suggestions that if microscopic life could have evolved in the harsh climate of Mars, then that substantially increases the likelihood of life elsewhere in the universe. In fact, there may be evidence of extraterrestrial life within our own solar system.

The most likely place where man will discover life within our solar system would be where water is (or at least believed to be) in abundance. The only other place in our solar system where water may be in abundance is on Jupiter's moon Europa. Europa appears to be covered with ice, but many astronomers believe that there is likely a liquid ocean beneath that ice, kept liquid by the heat emissions and gravitational forces of Jupiter. That being said, it is very possible that some simple aquatic life forms may exist on Europa.

A suggested NASA exploration mission, which may only be a rumor, might answer this question once and for all. The proposed mission would be to launch an unmanned probe to specifically land on Europa's icy surface, drop a heating element on the ice to melt down through the ice until the liquid ocean is reached. Then, the probe would launch an unmanned mini submarine probe to explore the oceanic depths of Europa. There are no details of if or when this mission might occur at the time this discussion was written, but the outcome of such a mission could substantially impact the way many people see the universe.

Number 1: "Man is created in the image of God"

Many religions throughout the world subscribe to a belief system the embraces the existence of one or more gods.

The Modern Paradigm of Liberty

Interestingly, despite the fact that many of these religions subscribe to very different philosophies, there does seem to be a consistent theme, that their image of their gods all appear to have very human characteristics, if not completely human. The obvious question is, if our characteristics are a product of natural evolutionary development, not unlike all other animals, then why would something metaphysical resemble us? Or do we resemble it? No matter, that is irrelevant to this point.

For the most common conventional faiths in the United States, those of Judeo-Christian origin, the basic belief is that man is specifically created in God's image. But who is God? God is the creator of everything. He is all-powerful. He is all-knowing. He is perfect. He is the greatest thing ever to exist and will ever exist in the universe for all time. Now, while the belief in such a being is by no means arrogant, to believe that you are created in the image of something so awesome, powerful and majestic is the epitome of arrogance.

The Electoral College

In the wake of the 2000 Presidential election fiasco, the press, the government and the citizenry all called for some form of election reform to prevent such a controversial victory from ever occurring again. The opponents of the current system argued that a candidate could win the Presidency without a majority of the popular vote. Further, the Electoral College coupled with the post-election conditions within the state of Florida challenged the whole "one person one vote" principle, which some believe is a fundamental characteristic of a democracy.

First, let us examine the value of the Electoral College and the reason why the founders articulated this in the U.S. Constitution in the first place. We have to remember that the United States is less like an individual country and more like a collection of countries under one macro governmental model. That being said, there are obvious concerns when it comes to the elections of federal representation. The Senate is easy, two Senators per State. The House of Representatives is also pretty easy, distribution of representation based on population. But, the Presidency is unique.

If the Presidency were to be solely elected on popular vote, campaigning would only occur in those areas of the federation that are densely populated. Furthermore, there would be no incentive for a candidate to campaign, appease or even act in the best interest of the sparse regions of the federation, especially if he/she could gain favor in the denser regions at the expense of the sparser regions. As a result, the more populous states would have a substantially unfair control over the Presidency.

With the Electoral College, each state ultimately plays a significant role in the election of a President. As a result, a candidate cannot win the election without a majority of Electoral votes. That means the candidates must campaign nationally in order to secure sufficient Electoral votes for victory. In a federation, the concept of "one person one vote" cannot apply to federal positions elected at-large as this illustrates tyranny of the majority.

This is not to say that the Electoral College is not flawed. To date, the assignment of Electoral votes within a state is assigned to the candidate with the most votes and NOT the majority, which can occur if there are more than two candidates. Therefore, in theory, ALL electoral votes for a state

The Modern Paradigm of Liberty

can be assigned to a candidate that the majority of a state did not vote for.

The fairest solution is to distribute Electoral votes within each state proportionately based on the percentage of the popular vote within that state. So, in the case of Florida where 25 Electoral votes were in dispute, the popular vote was almost even. This would have meant each candidate would have received at least 12 Electoral votes and the last remaining vote would have gone to the ultimate popular vote winner. If Florida adopted this model, Al Gore would have been President on Wednesday, November 8th, 2000 and the election would have been a memory instead of a controversy.

But wait, if **all** states employed the same proportionate strategy, would Al Gore still receive enough Electoral Votes? In New York, where George Bush received approximately 37% of the popular vote, he received ZERO Electoral votes. Again, the assignment of the Electoral votes does not represent the opinions of the state. If the Electoral votes were to be divided proportionately by percentage of popular vote across the 16 candidates (yes there were 16 candidates) then George Bush would have received 259 Electoral votes, Al Gore would have received 258, and the remaining Electoral votes would have been spread across the remaining candidates.

But wait, there's more! According to the 12th Amendment, if no candidate receives a majority of the Electoral votes, which is 270, then the vote goes to the House of Representatives for an immediate ballot. Since representation in the House of Representatives is by population, then this seems rational.

But wait, there's even more! Although this is specifically enumerated within the 12th Amendment, an argument can be reasonably made that such a vote would violate the separation of powers within the federal government as one branch of government would be asserting power over another.

In the case of the 2000 Presidential election, there were actually 16 candidates. What if instead of the popular vote being somewhat evenly split among two candidates it was rather evenly distributed across three, or four or five? Then, we are back to the House of Representatives.

This problem can be solved and avoided with a General Primary election that occurs between the respective Party Primary elections and Election Day. During the General Primary, all 16 candidates would be on the ballot and those two candidates who receive the two highest popular votes would be in the final election. In addition, since the General Primary would not be the final election, then voters may be more inclined to vote for a third-party candidate.

So what do we do? First, the Electoral College should be a fairer representation of popular opinion, so proportionate allotment of Electoral votes based on popular vote within a state should be instated.

Secondly, the current total number of Electoral votes is 538, requiring 270 votes to win. Therefore, the election could still end in a 269-269 tie. To prevent this, there should be an odd number of Electoral votes available so that a tie would be impossible.

Finally, there should only be two candidates in the final Presidential election who are chosen by the results of the General Primary. Since the final election would have only two candidates, then there would never be a case where a candidate would not receive a majority of Electoral votes, which eliminates the likelihood of involving the House of Representatives.

In any case, without any kind of Presidential election reform, we will be stuck with a model that misrepresents the collective will of the people and be forever locked into the existing two-party system.

Voter Nullification

Okay, we have all seen elections where we don't like any of the candidates. In a two-party system, we feel trapped voting for the candidate who supports the issues that mean the most to us personally. But too often, these candidates also take positions on other issues that we staunchly disagree with.

The problem is, both the Republicans and the Democrats sponsor candidates who support the traditional blanket platform of the party they represent. Despite the fact that the political party affiliation of most people is one of these two parties; the reality is most people aren't extremists.

If political beliefs were a bell curve and Democrats/Liberals were on one side and Republicans/Conservatives were on the other, most of us would probably fall somewhere in the middle. Think about it and ask yourself, how many people do you know have both some liberal views and some conservative views?

That being said, how could either candidate be representative of the majority?

Even worse, what if you just don't like any of the candidates? What is the recourse for the people in our democratic electoral process to express their disdain for all the candidates? Do you abstain your vote by not voting at all? And if so, then those who do vote will still elect a candidate whom you don't like.

So, what do you do? Unfortunately, you can't do anything. Quite frankly, that sucks and a democratic process should allow for the people as a whole to be collectively heard under these circumstances.

Could there be another option? In this author's opinion, there is. I must admit, this suggestion is not an original idea of this author, but rather one suggested in the motion picture **Brewster's Millions**. In the movie, Richard Pryor's character posed this same thesis for the New York City mayoral election. As a result, he lobbied the electorate to add "*None of the Above*" as a write-in vote. That's perfect.

More pragmatically, the ballot should include an option to abstain your vote, i.e. "none of the above". In this case, the voters can at least communicate to government, the media and the people that they disapprove of all candidates running in the election. The majority vote would still win. If the abstained votes should receive the majority, then none of the candidates would win and there would have to be a special election with entirely new candidates. The people have spoken.

Consumption Taxation

The debate of taxation in the United States is as old as the nation itself. Most people don't like paying taxes, and who can blame them. But the reality is, a government with responsibilities to protect its citizens from its enemies, provide executive/administrative leadership and services, and maintain the system of government, must impose taxation as necessary.

But the biggest complaint about taxation tends to be less about the percentage and more about waste. On January 27, 2002, Investigative Reporter John Stossel broadcast a special on taxation and government waste titled "Mr. Stossel Goes to Washington." Of many things, the program concluded the following:

- One out of every three tax dollars spent is lost to government waste.
- Americans pay more in taxes than we do in food, clothing and shelter combined.

- The average worker works until the month of May just to pay off their taxes.

While many may dispute Mr. Stossel's findings, few would argue at the amount of taxation that exists in the United States and the lack of fairness of taxation across the citizenry. One of the principle reasons why most people are so oblivious to the amount of taxation that occurs is because of all the hidden taxes that exist. These taxes include: taxes on cable TV, water, telephone, hotel accommodations, etc. The amount of individual taxes are seemingly endless, most of which are covert and depend on either the ignorance or indifference of the consumer.

And then there are income taxes. Is that fairly applied? Not by a long shot. Both sides of the political isle try to make themselves out to be the champion of better taxation for Americans and accuse the other side of bad tax policies. Arguments like "Tax and Spend" or "Tax Cuts for the Rich" are often thrown around. Both of these arguments are flawed at the core.

"Tax and Spend" is the action of government whether they tax a little or a lot. People would not mind a "tax and spend" government too much if the benefits to society can truly be quantified and waste of tax dollars was minimal.

As for "Tax Cuts for the Rich", this is merely a ploy to sway the opinions of the non-wealthy, specifically the poor. The fact is the wealthy often don't pay taxes in the traditional paradigm like most Americans. They have personal companies and various tax shelters to reduce their tax liability substantially. So, the basic tax rules that apply to the vast majority of Americans don't apply to the wealthy. Therefore, suggesting that income tax cuts that are targeted at benefiting the middle and lower class, are "tax cuts for the rich" is simply nonsense.

With all the countless hidden taxes and nuances in the tax laws, is there a fair and balanced way to have taxation, know exactly how much we are paying at all times, and be fairly applied to all people equally? Yes, there is. Taxation should be based solely on consumption, i.e. Sales and Use[1] Taxes. All other taxes should be repealed.

The logic is simple. The more money you have, the more you spend; the more you spend, the more taxes you pay. The less money you have, the less you spend; the less you spend, the less taxes you pay. It is so simple, a child can understand it.

If Sales and Use Taxes were the only taxes of all levels of government, there would have be a Federal Sales/Use Tax in addition to the State Sales/Use Tax. The bad news for the people is that, between the two taxes, the combined Sales Tax rate would likely exceed 20%, if not 30% per purchase.

The good news is that people would not pay any income tax and would never have to file a tax return again. Even better, people would be in greater control of their taxation as sales tax is a percentage of the purchase price, so the cheaper the product, the lower the tax. People could then budget for their taxes. Finally, they would know exactly how much taxes they are paying and at what rate. Armed with this knowledge, the people would be more inclined and sufficiently prepared to hold government accountable for their tax dollars.

There is also an added benefit. If all taxation is based on consumption taxes, then those people spending money in the United States who do not pay income taxes (such as tourists, illegal aliens, people working off-the-books, etc.) would bear more of the tax burden.

For government, this is both good and bad. The bad includes various daunting efforts. Imposing consumption taxes would require a standardization of what is and is not taxable across the entire country. There currently is a charge by the National Conference of Commissioners on Uniform State Laws (NCCUSL) to standardize sales taxation, as a product of the former Advisory Commission on Electronic Commerce. There goal is to standardize sales taxation as a measure towards asserting sales tax jurisdiction on e-commerce, where the average American can otherwise engage in sales tax evasion.

In addition, the government would need to dismantle the Internal Revenue Service (and the State level equivalent) as it is currently defined. If all taxation is based entirely on consumption and collected primarily at the point of purchase, virtually all taxes could be collected immediately (mostly likely weekly, monthly, or quarterly), and transferred to government accounts via electronic funds transfer through a clearing house, not unlike direct deposit for paychecks.

Third, government would find budgeting substantially more challenging as forecasting income taxes is much easier that forecasting sales taxes. Sales taxes depend entirely on consumer behavior and are subject to their perceptions of the market, the economy, and the nation as a whole.

Finally, government would lose a great deal of control over the people as the people would be in almost complete control of how much taxes they pay. But isn't that what the founders wanted, a government controlled by the people and accountable to the people? Establishing a consumption tax paradigm allows for the people to retain more control of governance.

The good news for government is that they would substantially reduce the overhead of maintaining the Internal Revenue Service (and the State level equivalent), including all the administrative and enforcement therein. Also, they would receive most tax dollars almost immediately, without the concern of having to issue tax return refunds. What government receives is theirs.

Further, if government needed to increase or decrease taxes, they would be able to impose those changes in a very timely and efficient manner. Finally, successful governance would truly be linked to the economy. The more people spend, the better it is for government, the economy and the country as a whole.

Plus, if the federal government ever wanted to quickly stimulate the economy during a period of recession, they could easily impose a temporary moratorium on the federal sales tax. States could coordinate their efforts as well. Look what happens when New York has a sales tax free week. Shoppers go nuts.

Additionally, government can still augment their tax revenue by charging fees for service. Typical examples would be buses, subways, trains, toll booths, park fees, etc. These are also considered consumption taxes that would only apply to the people who use these services of government.

What Americans want and need is a taxation solution that is simple, effective and fair. This approach satisfies all three. The taxation of the American people has gradually grown into a convoluted multi-tiered bureaucracy, which even government experts cannot agree upon its interpretation.

In the end, I'm afraid, we will likely be stuck with this same taxation paradigm that we are currently subject to as it is very unlikely that government would voluntarily return this much power to the people. But maybe we deserve it. After all, we are the people who gave government this power in the first place, thus we reap what we sow.

[1] *Note: Use taxes are equal to the Sales Tax rate, but are collected not at the point of purchase, but paid directly to a state. An example would be if a person purchased an item out of state, where the retailer at the point of purchase does not collect the sales tax. The buyer is required by law to pay the use tax to their home state once the product in brought back to their home state. This is the debate behind the taxation of e-commerce.*

The Stock Market

Okay, we have all seen them. We turn on CNN-FN, CNBC, and all the other shows that have all the **experts** talking about what is happening in the stock market and what they **think** will happen in the market next. We, the viewer, are supposed to see this and assume there is some value to their statements and, as a result, make what we believe to be educated decisions based on their information so that we can win in the market. If so, why did so many people lose so much money in recent years? Of course, all the market analysts can tell you now how we lost the money, as hindsight is 20/20 vision, but where were they before we lost our money?

It is actual quite simple, these so-called stock market analyst and experts really don't know what they are talking about as it relates to future investments. The fact is, the best information today cannot tell you anything more than what has already happened, period. Proof of this is in the disclaimers presented whenever these stock funds promote themselves. They always include the disclaimer that "past performance is not indicative of future performance" or some other paraphrase meaning the same thing.

Prior to the market *correction* which put the market in the state it is was in 2002, all the analysts were talking about how great everything is and how it will get better. It was the analysts who over valued the Internet and the dot-com stocks, which over valued the NASDAQ. Now, after the bottom fell out, there is of course no shortage of analysts and experts to tell us what happened. Of course they can tell us what happened, because it already happened!

Even more amusing is what happens when an "analyst" *predicts* something that actually does come true. This is such a rarity that is the cause for celebration, which these stock analysis shows jump all over in an effort to validate their guesswork to the viewing public as legitimate analysis.

See for yourself and be objective. Watch these analysts with an objective eye. You will very quickly see many of these experts say one thing while many others saying the complete opposite. If this truly were a science based on facts, algorithms and empirical data to forecast future outcomes, shouldn't they all say the exact same thing? Well, they don't.

In fact, they are all over the spectrum. This is why they always advise us to **diversify**, so that collectively we can do okay, which is just a product of pure luck. The television news program 20/20 publicly presented proof of this hypothesis. They had a program where a chimpanzee threw darts at a page of stocks to create a portfolio that could perform as well, if not better, than any money manager.

So, what can we count on if not the analysts? Simple, we can count on the one thing that has been predictable throughout the centuries; human stupidity as it relates to the panic of the masses.

What happens if a company reports that it will fall short of forecasted earnings, or even warns of it? Simple, people think the stock is not worth as much as it was and dump it. Then, the stock price falls. In reality, the company was exactly the same company it was before the earnings report, so why is it valued less? It is valued less simply because people think it is. But the average amateur trader tends to be short-sighted when it comes to the market.

Look at most major stocks that have dropped significantly in a short time because of an earnings report. Within a few months, the majority of them have regained much of what they lost, if not all of it. This is because the emotional panic that people have has no real long lasting impact on a stock or market as a whole. Only real problems, like true changes in the marketplace (such as a shift in consumer activity) or criminal activity (*Enron and Worldcom are you listening*) truly have a long lasting impact on the stock market.

No, this is not a full proof plan to win at the market, it is just common sense based on the only truly predictable influence on the stock market. Invest with this in mind, and you'll probably do okay.

With that aside, what really turns this author's stomach is the notion that we **should** invest in the market **now** for the good of the economy and the good of the country, using patriotism as the basis of the argument. This promotion of investing is an attempt to get people to invest and spend money to stimulate the economy and get us out of the recession. Again, shear nonsense.

The week of September 11, 2001, the stock market was unexpectedly closed for most of that week. Despite the national crisis, businesses were still opened, products where still delivered to their retailers, and people still made purchases. Did the economy go into a tailspin? Nope. This shows that our economy does not need the stock market nearly as much as people think we need it.

Sure, companies use stock as a means to raise capital for investment in their company so they can grow, but that takes a back seat to the actual day-to-day activity of a business and the consumers. The week of September 11th proved that. September 11th also proves the panic theory. The first few days after the market reopened was a roller coaster ride driven entirely by consumer panic. Only those who did not succumb to the panic, or worked it to their advantage, didn't suffer.

In the months that followed, the government, the news media and the market analysts were all telling us that it is our patriotic duty to reinvest in the market. That's a cheap shot. People are in this financial mess because these analysts and everyone who perpetuates their useless drivel caused this mess by over valuing the Internet and the Dot-Coms in the first place, as well as providing so-called *expert* advice entirely from platitude. They created they mess and they want us to bail them out.

I say, let them suffer. Put your money were it really counts, in investments that mean something and are sound. These include real estate, savings bonds, T-bills, and other tangible investments that are *real* and are the best investments for the long term. Finally, if you really want to do something patriotic with your money and stimulate the economy, buy something.

The Economics of School Vouchers

Many opponents of the school voucher concept use the separation of church and state argument as the unconstitutional basis for their opposition. While there is some legitimacy to the separation violation, the issue of whether or not school vouchers should be issued can be substantially argued independent of the religious debate.

First, there are concerns that public funding in the form of school vouchers routed to schools tied to religious beliefs violates the tenet of the separation of church and state. The separation of church and state would be violated if the school voucher program where unfairly applied towards private schools that are religious based versus private schools that are not religious based or vice versa. If the voucher program is universally and equally applied to any and all private schools, whether they preach religion or not, then in this author's opinion, the separation violation argument is voided.

However, there is a more significant concern with the school voucher program that cannot be so easily dismissed, and that issue is economically based. It is important to point out that public and private schools operate under two separate and distinct administrative models. Public schools use the Public Administration model while private schools follow more of a Business Administration model. This distinction is critical to the debate as the basic missions of these two paradigms are fundamentally different at their core.

At the root of all business models, the ultimate mission is to have revenue exceed expenses to generate a profit, i.e. "***to make money***." This basic mission differentiates business models from public administration because all public administrative models operate under a different basic mission, "***to serve the people***." Since these basic missions are completely incompatible, comparing the two models is like comparing apples and oranges.

Understanding that private schools operate under a business model, it becomes much clearer to the average observer why the school voucher concept falls apart. For example, let us assume that annual tuition for a private school is $2000 prior to the introduction of the school voucher program. Those who can afford this tuition are currently paying the $2000. Those that cannot afford the $2000 tuition are herded into the public schools.

The Modern Paradigm of Liberty

In theory, if government issued a $1000 voucher per year per student, then many families who could not afford the $2000 tuition before could now afford it because their expense is only $1000 out of pocket as the total tuition becomes attainable to substantially more of the public as a product of the voucher and personal contribution.

In our example, this would put private school with in the financial reach of substantially more people than before. However, the number of private schools and seats within them will likely remain the same. Knowing that private schools are a business, you can apply the basic business economic principle of **supply** and **demand**.

With the issuance of school vouchers, there would be a substantial increase in demand by the customer base while the supply remains essentially the same. Supply and demand dictates that if demand increases while supply remains the same, then there will be an increase in price.

What would likely happen with private schools is that tuition prices would increase, most likely by the voucher amount. In our example, the private school would increase the annual tuition from $2,000 to $3000. Therefore, those who could afford the original $2000 tuition before would still be able to afford the new $3000 tuition when they combine their personal contribution with the school voucher, and those who could not afford the original $2000 tuition would still not be able to afford the new $3000 tuition even with the $1,000 school voucher as the net personal contribution would still be $2000.

In the end, everyone is back where they started, less of the government budget is appropriated to the already struggling public school system, taxes would have increase to offset this debacle and the private schools stand to make substantially more money without any investment or risk all at the expense of the taxpayer.

Finally, those in the lowest economic conditions would be hurt the most. Much of the poor would never be able to afford private schools even with vouchers, so the private school option would always remain unattainable and the poor would be left to a public school system that has been subjected to diminished funding as school vouchers divert public funding to the private sector.

Taxation without Representation

One of the founding principles that fueled the American Revolution was the notion of "no taxation without representation." The historical significance behind this position can be researched and justified within its own right. For the purposes of this discussion, it is this author's opinion that no taxation without representation is simple and an obvious characteristic in a free society.

On a federal level, this concept is protected by Article I, Section 8 of the United States Constitution, where it states that Congress shall have power to lay and collect taxes. Since both Houses of Congress consists of representatives elected by the people, there is no dispute that federal taxation only occurs as a product of democracy.

But what about at the state level? Sure, if you live and work in a state that levies taxes on its residents and you have the right to vote, the same would seem to apply as in the federal model. But is that the only scenario? **No**.

What if you live in one state but work in a neighboring state? What ends up happening is that you have to pay income tax to the state you reside in (less the fact that you don't work there) and pay income tax to the state you work in (less the fact that you don't live there).

Now, there is seldom any attention brought to this issue, as this is often a financial wash. But that does not change the fact that this model overtly violates a basic principle conceived by the founders, which fueled the revolution. If you live in New York where you can vote for New York representation, but you work in Connecticut where you *cannot* vote for Connecticut representation, what justifies Connecticut to assert income tax jurisdiction on you?

How can you hold Connecticut government leaders accountable for your taxation and appropriation of those dollars if you cannot vote for them? To put it simply, you can't. This is overt taxation without representation and it must be stopped to honor the true spirit of the founders.

The solution is actually quite simple, no state should be able to assert income tax jurisdiction on non-residents. Additionally, all states would assert income tax jurisdiction on their residents only. Such revision would be the equivalent of current taxation on residents who both live and work within the state, regardless of where they actually work.

The Modern Paradigm of Liberty

This same model should also apply to local municipal income taxes. Why should someone living in White Plains, NY pay any New York City income taxes if they only work there? They can't vote for those elected city officials and asserting tax jurisdiction on them again violates this tenet.

This model ultimately works in the best interest of all. For the most part, the taxation within each tax jurisdiction (state or local) would probably be a wash, with few exceptions. The processing of personal income taxes by each state becomes a lot simpler, the process for filing personal taxes for many people becomes a lot simpler and the people will know that all their income taxes and appropriations are a product of their direct representation by which they can hold accountable.

The catch; for those jurisdictions that result in a loss of tax revenue, they will have to raise taxes to their constituency and/or businesses, or otherwise find additional sources of revenue. If their constituency disapproves of the increases in taxes and service fees, they can at least hold their elected officials accountable.

As for usage of municipal/government services by residents outside of the jurisdiction, fees for service regardless of where you are from should fund them (example: toll booths/roads, train fair, subway fair, bus fair, etc.). Charging everyone fees for service is equally and evenly applied. If you don't like the fee for service, don't use the service. This can be used as a means to collect revenue from out-of-town visitors, such as commuters using a toll booth.

Now there is likely some concern that the suburbs or the more affluent neighborhoods would have lower taxation while these people commute into the major metropolitan areas (example: living in Greenwich, CT and working in New York City). Here, it would seem that the wealthy would somehow escape the burden of New York City tax and the tax burden would have to be shouldered by those in New York City who may not be able to afford it.

This is partially alleviated by the fee for service option. Further this is also alleviated by corporate taxation. If these people are working for companies within the jurisdiction of a municipality, then that municipality can assert tax jurisdiction on the companies accordingly by increasing corporate taxes.

Finally, a substantial percentage of the financial support of the lower levels of government comes from taxation at the state level, i.e. the state appropriates tax dollars to the areas of the state that need it most.

But, in this author's opinion, this whole argument is actually moot. In reality, if all income taxation were to disappear and consumption taxes were modified to pick up the balance, then the amount of individual taxation would truly be in the control of the citizen. This is explored in an earlier discussion titled *Consumption Taxation*.

The Politics of Heaven

Religion has been around for thousands of years, including the popular denominations of Judaism and Christianity. While traditional religious practitioners subscribe to the notion that the origins of religion are seated in divine providence, more progressive contemporary thinkers have argued that religion is the product of man's creation.

While this discussion will not address the origins of religion in general, it will focus on a central point within many religions, Heaven. Most major religions subscribe to the notion of an eternal afterlife where we would live as one with our God in paradise. Ascension to such paradise is normally the product of *good* or *favorable* religious behavior. In any case, the end result is a reward of eternal happiness in *paradise*. But what is paradise?

Is paradise a universal term? Does everyone perceive paradise to be the same thing or is the perception of paradise subjective to the individual? If you subscribe to the doctrine of faith wholeheartedly, then your perception of paradise should be consistent across your belief system. But, since belief systems vary widely, there is no universal consensus on what paradise is. So, we should begin with the definition from the Merriam-Webster dictionary:

Paradise: **1 a :** Eden **b :** an intermediate place or state where the righteous departed await resurrection and judgment **c :** Heaven; **2 :** a place or state of bliss, felicity, or delight[1]

The notion of paradise with respect to Eden and Heaven is pretty consistent with the biblical reference as the Bible probably illustrates one of the oldest specific instances of the concept. But the more generic definition of paradise suggests that paradise is, in reality, subjective to the faith practiced, if not the individual as it is a personal state of bliss.

But let us assume that Judeo-Christian monotheism is the benchmark. Then, Heaven is the place where good religious people go when they die, while those whom are not considered to be of good religious standing are banished to eternal damnation.

But is Heaven all that desirable? Let us examine Heaven objectively as a society. First, Heaven must be considered a society since the souls of people comprise Heaven's population. Since people of faith believe that the soul is the essence of who we are, then the souls of people make up the citizenry of Heaven.

The Modern Paradigm of Liberty

So how are these citizens governed? Well, there is no question among religious individuals that the leader in Heaven is God. If that is true, how did God obtain such authority? Was he elected? Is he accountable to the citizenry by way of an electoral process, a constitution, or societal law? **No**. God is a self-appointed leader whose word *is* law. He is unelectable, unaccountable and irremovable.

So what happens if the collective population of Heaven decides that God is not serving them in their best interests? What is their recourse? Can they invoke change? Can they question their leaders? Can they peaceably assemble? Do they have a representative legislative body that will hear their grievances? **No**. God's word is law, and if you don't like it you can go to Hell, quite literally.

Further, the actions of God throughout the Old Testament are also questionable with respect to the type of governance he provides. Countless cases, including the destruction of Sodom and Gomorrah as well as Noah's flood are examples of God's wraith. But more specifically, God punished those whom *he* subjectively considered to be sinners. He arbitrarily decided who lives and dies merely at his whim and discretion.

Given the above, what kind of society is Heaven? Quite obviously, the political structure of Heaven is a totalitarian autocracy where the self-appointed leader has absolute authority. All citizens of that society must comply with any law dictated by authority without question. Finally, the societal duty of every citizen is to *serve* God. Serve? What does that imply? Slavery perhaps?

These are somewhat harsh terms to describe Heaven and God's governance. Is it accurate? Let us again examine some definitions from the Merriam-Webster dictionary:

Totalitarian: **1 a** : of or relating to centralized control by an autocratic leader or hierarchy : Authoritarian, Dictatorial; *especially* : Despotic **b** : of or relating to a political regime based on subordination of the individual to the state and strict control of all aspects of the life and productive capacity of the nation especially by coercive measures (as censorship and terrorism)[2]

Autocracy: **1** : the authority or rule of an autocrat; **2** : government in which one person possesses unlimited power; **3** : a community or state governed by autocracy[3]

Clearly, according to traditional faiths, God possesses unlimited power in Heaven. Clearly, there is centralized control around God's authority. Clearly, the governance of Heaven asserts subordination of individuals to the service of God, a God who requires a strict control of all aspects of their existence. Clearly, God's methods to control the people subjects violators of his law to eternal torment. If that is not control and intimidation using the coercive measures of censorship and terrorism, what is?

By design, the society of Heaven is very contradictory to that of the contemporary United States. In the U.S., we have numerous basic rights of any free citizen, including the right to practice *any* religious belief system, effect positive change in our society, and hold our governmental leaders accountable.

That is the society we have all come to cherish as Americans. We have sacrificed countless American lives on the altar of freedom in defense of our individual liberties and our way of life. The Amendments to the U.S. Constitution guarantees these basic inalienable liberties which apparently do not exist in Heaven in any form.

So when presented with the argument by religious leaders that the "only way to Heaven is to know God and/or Jesus," we need to be asking ourselves if Heaven is where we want to go at all. Better yet, is Hell a better place to be than Heaven?

Consider that the Bible, in a very real sense, is a collective piece of marketing literature for God, Jesus, and Heaven in general. Like any other marketing literature, its efforts to sell their message is subjectively and intentionally presented in a positive light to the consumer, while simultaneously undermining and discrediting the competition (Hell) in the eyes of the consumer. Therefore, it should come as no surprise that Hell is illustrated as an undesirable place to be. But is it?

Consider this; a totalitarian society exists where the ruler is unelected, unaccountable and irremovable. The ruler has absolute authority over everyone in that society. As long as you are willing to serve the ruler without question and accept your place in servitude without individual liberties, free expression, and the like, you will enjoy that society. But, a group of citizens opted to challenge that authority in an effort to assert their individuality, freedoms and liberties, and are considered to be traitors to that society. The question is; is this a description of the Fall from Grace or the American Revolution?

So where do you want to go, Heaven or Hell? Better yet, why does there have to be only two options? Why can't enough souls break off from either Heaven or Hell and form their own metaphysical society based on the notion of individual liberties and freedoms, emulating the United States? Or, better yet, if Hell is the place of eternal damnation, what if the collective souls in Hell were to unite and overthrow Satan and establish a free society in Hell? Maybe this has already happened. Since we have no direct communication with Heaven or Hell, we won't know until we get there.

As an Atheist, I don't believe in either Heaven or Hell. For those readers who are devoutly religious and strictly believe in both, then you have already concluded where I am going. Maybe you're right and I'm wrong. But I'll tell you this; I would rather be in Hell for an eternity then to serve in Heaven for a single day. Besides, with my commitment to a free society, I would likely rally the other tortured souls in Hell and lead an insurrection to establish a free society.

Clearly, Satan is not *all-powerful* and can be defeated, as he was cast out of Heaven. With enough souls rallying behind me, we could eventually succeed at independence. Hey, if a sentence in Hell is for an eternity, I'll have an unlimited amount of time on my hands and plenty of torture souls willing to follow. At least I won't be bored.

[1] *www.m-w.com, Search word **Paradise***
[2] *www.m-w.com, Search word **Totalitarian***
[3] *www.m-w.com, Search word **Autocracy***

The Ten Commandments

There has been recent debate about the display of the "Ten Commandments" on public buildings, including courthouses, schools, and the like. The basic argument by supporters is that the culture of Western Civilization is rooted in the laws of the Ten Commandments. Further, they assert that the Ten Commandments is a historical document and to exclude them from the public would be to deny history. Perhaps there is some truth to that argument, but there are many more questions that need to be researched and answered before widespread and universal public acceptance can occur.

First, the Bible, and to a lesser extent the Ten Commandments, have culturally influenced the course of Europe and the United States throughout the centuries, for good and for bad. Most of the "Sunday" laws, such as limitations of the sale of alcohol, are all tied to the Sabbath. But did the founding fathers of the United States really want the

Ten Commandments to supersede American law? Further, were their formal constitutional actions in support of the Ten Commandments or to the contrary?

Let us examine the Ten Commandments with respect to the First Amendment to the U.S. Constitution. The First Amendment, conceived and unanimously approved by the founders directly reputes the first three of the Ten Commandments.

The First Commandment specifically asserts that "thou shalt have none other gods before me." But the First Amendment to the U.S. Constitution clearly states that "Congress shall make no law respecting an establishment of religion, **or prohibiting the free exercise thereof**." The founders ensured that government would **never** be allowed to pass any law that would restrict the practice of any religion, regardless of the religion or deity worshiped. This means that Americans have the basic right to worship any deity or deities they wish, which reputes the tenet that "thou shalt have none other gods before me."

The Second Commandment (according to Protestant and Jewish interpretation) states that "thou shalt not make unto me any ungraven image." While the First Amendment does not specifically enumerate that the people have the right to create any images they wish, the interpretation of free speech has a long standing history of supporting freedom of expression in art, literature and personal expression. Free expression of any images created by man guaranteed by the First Amendment would be in repudiation to the Second Commandment.

The Third Commandment states that "thou shalt not take the name of thy God in vain." In short, this is a prohibition on blasphemy. Well, the First Amendment not only ensures religious freedom, but it specifically asserts that Congress shall make no law "abridging the freedom of speech." Therefore, Congress would not have any power to criminalize blasphemy as it is free speech by its very nature. Again, the First Amendment overtly reputes the Third Commandment.

Interesting, the Fourth Commandment, which forbids work on the Sabbath, includes specific language restricting the work of slaves, although more politically correct translations substitute "*servants*" for "*slaves*". In addition, the Tenth Commandment, which is often referred to as forbidding coveting, includes slaves among the neighbor's possessions. What is interesting is that there is no condemnation of slavery at all in the Ten Commandments, but an accommodation for it.

Slavery is contrary to a free society and, although the founding fathers did not abolish slavery at the birth of the nation, the Thirteenth Amendment to the U.S. Constitution ratified in 1865 does abolish slavery. To suggest slavery as an acceptable practice in contemporary American society would be absurd, but apparently is within the acceptance of the Ten Commandments.

But let us assume that none of the previous contradictions exist. Would it be okay to post the Ten Commandments then? Well, the first question that would need to be answered is: *Which version?* There are three generally accepted versions of the Ten Commandments, the Jewish, the Catholic and the Protestant. The differences are significant enough to suggest that posting any one of these three will breach the religious establishment restriction with respect to the other two.

Furthermore, contrary to common belief, the Ten Commandments are *not* a list of one-through-ten appearing verbatim in the Bible, regardless of the version. Rather, they are much wordier than people realize. For the full length and content of the text for the Ten Commandments, refer to *Exodus 34:1 through 34:32* and *Deuteronomy 5:6 through 5:22*. Depending on the version of these books referenced, the language and translations will vary.

In any case neither Exodus nor Deuteronomy lists the commandments in a quick one-through-ten summary. To post the Ten Commandments and represent them accurately, could only be done by taking the oldest version of the text, the Jewish Torah, and translate these two sections to their closest English translations and then display both the Exodus and Deuteronomy versions in their entirety.

Now, assuming we ignore the conflicts between the Ten Commandments and the United States Constitution and assuming that the entire text of both Exodus & Deuteronomy were properly translated, what would be the remaining barrier to displaying the Ten Commandments? Historical accuracy.

It is widely accepted in academic circles of Egyptology that the events surrounding enslavement of Jews in Egypt, the story of Moses, the Ten Commandments, the 40 year journey, etc., are **NOT** historical events. In fact, virtually all archaeological evidence points to the contrary. See for yourself, pick up almost any non-religious book about ancient Egypt and there would be almost no reference to any event that could be even remotely linked to the biblical stories.

Also, while the Bible tells these stories with intricate details, it frequently refers to Pharaoh and/or the King of Egypt, but never once mentions his name. The intentional omission of this otherwise critical fact should be suspect itself, as it might be an intentional effort to conceal the truth or prevent anyone from challenging the validity of these stories.

However, the Hollywood rendition of The Ten Commandments, starring Charlton Heston, depicts the period to be during the reigns of Seti I and Ramses II. Today, archaeologists know a great deal about Ancient Egypt, particularly the 19th Dynasty, which included the reigns of Seti I and Ramses II, with no evidence to suggest that any of these events might have occurred.

This raises serious questions on the historical accuracy of the events and the document itself. For government to sponsor something that has virtual no historical basis in fact, particularly in educational venues, is irresponsible.

For the Ten Commandments to be presented and taught in public schools, it would need to pass the test of historical research and accuracy, like any other event in history. Absent that, it can only be considered myth and treated in the same context as any other mythology, such as the polytheistic beliefs of Greco-Roman origin.

So we must ask ourselves, do we want to promote doctrines in public venues that support unconstitutional principles, making them contrary to the foundation and framework of contemporary freedom and liberty? If so, do we want to paraphrase the word of God so that it is convenient for us and politically correct? If so, do we want to present myth as fact without any historical credibility in educational venues?

If the answer to all these questions is "Yes", they we should post the Ten Commandments on public buildings. But since we are a society that likes to consider itself enlightened and intellectual, facts and *not* myth are what should be publicly sponsored and taught. But the Ten Commandments do have a place in our society, particularly for those who hold the content dear. These places include the home, the church and in Sunday school, but they do *NOT* include the public square.

Finally, any government sponsorship of the Ten Commandments is not merely a violation of the separation of church and state, it is a violation of freedom of religion. By sponsoring the Ten Commandments, government is asserting and sponsoring it as a universal societal legitimacy, particularly applying to those commandments relative to the Judeo-Christian God. This contradicts an individual's freedom of religion should he/she decide to practice some religion that does not subscribe to a Judeo-Christian God.

So, which supersedes which, the U.S. Constitution or the Ten Commandments? According to American Constitutional law, it is the U.S. Constitution, since the Ten Commandments have no legally binding power in the United States as they have **NEVER** been ratified into law at any level of government. Thus, any level of government that supports a public display of the Ten Commandments is not just in violation of the U.S. Constitution with respect to religious freedom, they are overtly undermining the U.S. Constitution, and THAT is simply un-American.

Special Note: *This essay was largely inspired by the following article:*
Zindler, Frank R. (2000 Spring) "**Hang 'em All – Completely!**"
American Atheist, Volume 38, Number 2, p12-p18.

School Prayer

Years ago prayer in public school was common. Being an Atheist, this author does not like that fact, but that does not change the reality. But as we grow as a society that celebrates religious freedom and continuously aspires towards an ideally free society, we must grow and accept newer liberties and freedoms that may not have been previously recognized, as well as shed any infringements of our rights that are rooted in the past. Such is the case of school prayer.

School prayer was often very Christian in context, typically reciting the "Lord's Prayer." Clearly, any endorsement of Christianity by government in public schools undermines other otherwise common religious beliefs, such as Judaism and Islam. Even further, it arguably violates the separation of church and state. The tables turned on school prayer with the landmark U.S. Supreme Court Case *Murray v. Curlett*, which outlawed forced prayer and Bible-reading in American public schools.

But religious Americans have not given up. Today, the charge is to have a "moment of silence and personal reflection" introduced into school, where some students can **choose** to pray. If the actions of the students during this moment of silence and personal reflection are **NOT** sponsored or lead by representatives or employees of government and are solely personal in nature, then it is this author's opinion that this would **not** violate a separation of church and state as any religious actions by the students would be totally self-motivated.

However, those of the religious mainstream need to be prepared and tolerant of those outside the religious mainstream who engage in atypical religious practices, such as Druidism, Wicca, or even the occult. The moment of silence and personal reflection should apply to all equally and without discrimination against any belief system whatsoever.

But is there still a place for open/group prayer in public school that would not violate the separation of church and state? Perhaps there is. The biggest concern by those who are charged with supporting the separation of church and state is that government should not sponsor any religious message. Inappropriate government sponsorship would likely be in the form of using government funded time, resources, and/or staff.

Government sponsored time begins at the start of the official school day and ends at the end of the official school

The Modern Paradigm of Liberty

day. Let us assume that these times are 8:00am and 3:00pm respectively for the purpose of this discussion. Between the hours of 8:00am and 3:00pm, it would be inappropriate for there to be any religious-based activity occurring on school grounds as that time is government sponsored, even if it were entirely student lead.

However, before 8:00am and after 3:00pm, the school simply becomes another public facility/venue where free people can peaceably assembly for any reason; students and teachers alike. This is not unlike a public meeting hall, a park or the steps of City Hall. If school prayer were to exist in the manner described above outside of government sponsored time, then the separation of church and state should still be satisfied.

But there is a Catch-22 here. If this model were allowed to exist, then **ANY** group should be allowed to meet and promote/practice their belief systems. A free society would have to allow this, even if the beliefs are unpopular, politically incorrect/ insensitive, or those of minority groups.

This could include groups supporting everything from gay-rights to neo-Nazism. Religious promoters can't have their cake and eat it too. They would have to accept the good with the bad, whichever they subjectively define as the *bad*. Government should be completely indifferent to all of these programs and neither support or denounce any of them, regardless of personal opinion or the passions of the mob.

So that is the compromise. It allows for those people who wish to express their religious beliefs in public school and with others who share their beliefs while maintaining a healthy respect for the separation of church and state. While this suggestion appears to be splitting hairs on the notion of exactly when prayer can and cannot occur in public school, the reality is there is a very big distinction between what are considered to be actions sponsored and lead by government and those lead by free people.

Science of the Soul

Many faiths teach their followers that the physical existence of humans is merely part of a life journey that extends beyond the mortal boundaries. They see the human body as a vessel for a deeper essence that is far greater than that of our physical being. For want of a better word, this is our "*soul*".

While religious scholars have debated the nature of the existence of such an entity, there is little discussion to whether or not such a thing even exists at all. The foundation of the debate always begins with the assumption that the soul exists without questioning the validity of that assumption. Perhaps the reason for this neglect in the analysis is due to a fear in the logical outcome, that humans may not have a soul at all.

But, let us assume that the soul exists. If it does, is it a living thing? In the conventional sense, the answer is plainly **No**. The reason is that all generally accepted definitions of life assert that the presence of genetic material must exist, even in the simplest form. If the soul contained genetic material, then advanced medical science would have found it by now. They haven't. So, the soul is not genetically based, or even based in matter. This leaves only one option left. Pure energy.

Therefore, if the soul exists and it is a form of life, then it must exist as life in a pure energy form. Historically, science takes a myopic view as it relates to finding the truth based on facts and empirical data. However, science is not so myopic when it comes to new discoveries. So, for the sake of this discussion, we will assume that life can exist in a pure energy form. Therefore, if neither the presence of genetic material nor even matter itself is a requirement of life, then life could only be defined by its behavior.

Thus, if something is alive, it must exercise the characteristics of life. So, what are the universal characteristics of all life? Simple, all life exhibits the same behavior: to consume enough nutrients to sustain its existence long enough to procreate/reproduce.

The next obvious question is: does the soul meet this criterion? Well, since science has yet to study a soul in its natural habitat, the findings are inconclusive. However, since we know that other forms of life exhibit metamorphic behavior, it is reasonable to assume that the soul is part of human life and the release of the soul at death is not unlike the release of a butterfly from the caterpillar's cocoon. That being said, we can take a leap of faith to assume that the soul exists and that it is alive for the continuance of this discussion.

Now, humans are clearly a complex life form. We have a very intricately evolved physical body, brain and mind. In a similar context, it would be reasonable to assume that the soul would be an equally complex pure energy life form. Now, we know that if complex *traditional* life exists, then simple *traditional* life exists. We can see the evidence of this statement with the examination of microscopic single cell organisms.

If we apply this same elementary reasoning process to pure energy life and the soul is a complex pure energy life form, then it stands to reason that there must exist pure energy life forms that qualify as simple life forms. So, if we apply the new definition of life, one based on behavior, and then examine energies that we know we can identify, measure, and study, then we should be able to locate at least one pure energy life form.

Based on the behavior definition of life, there is at least one obvious example of a simple form of life existing in a pure energy form that can be identified, measured and studied. The answer is **Fire**.

The very nature of fire exhibits the basic behavior of life. It consumes fuel and oxygen as its nutrients. The more it consumes, the bigger it gets. Eventually, a fire will get so big that it will shoot off sparks that often start other fires, which can be construed as reproduction.

Often when we talk about fire we use terms like "feeding the fire", "starving the fire", and "smothering the fire". Any fire expert will tell you that the behavior of fire is predictable to a point, but then can, at times, seems spontaneous, as if it were a wild animal. Without further discussion, this satisfies the basic criteria for pure energy life.

Now, this is not a suggestion that fire is a form of life, but based on the discussion above, it is more conceivable to believe that fire is a living thing than to believe that the soul is a living thing. Furthermore, we know for a fact that fire exists and can prove its existence, a test that the soul has yet to pass.

But to continue this discussion, let us still assume that the soul is alive and currently resides in the human body. We can deduce that while the soul remains in the body that the body contains the energy that makes up the soul, like a bottle. But when the bottle is opened or destroyed, i.e. death, the soul spills out. The obvious question should be; what force post mortem is keeping the soul together and/or maintaining the cohesion of the energy particles that comprise the soul?

Without such a container, force or cohesion, the energy would otherwise dissipate. There is no other reason to assume that the energy that makes up the soul would remain together and intact. Those who believe that the soul does exist and survives physical existence must answer this question to themselves with some basis in reality and common sense.

But again, let us assume that the soul is alive, resides in the human body and will maintain cohesion post mortem. What does it retain of the human experience? Many people and faiths believe that the soul is the essence of who they are, their consciousness, and that this consciousness will carry their experiences beyond this physical world.

We have all seen and heard stories of people who have "died and come back to life" where they claim that they have seen loved ones, walk down a tunnel of light, etc. Further, people who claim to be in communication with those who have "passed on" or "crossed over" have asserted a level of communication and understanding, suggesting that the culmination of a person's life experiences will be retained in the soul post mortem.

Forgive me for being so blunt, but that simply is not so. The modern understandings of the human brain by medical science can unquestionably prove certain key facts that undermine the soul belief. First, medical science can prove that it is the human brain that stores memories. This author is not a neurologist so the medical details are beyond the scope of this discussion, but suffice it to say the medicine is irrefutable.

Furthermore, medical science also knows for a fact that permanent brain damage results in permanent memory loss. Even further, medicine shows that the greater the brain damage, the greater the memory loss. Apply the basic mathematical principles of limits and asymptotes, we can reasonably conclude that complete destruction of a person's brain results in a complete loss of that person's memories. So, who are you without the sum total of your memories? Even a new born baby has some memories. Without any memories, you are nothing, a clean slate.

So, let us summarize. If your soul exists in the traditional sense, it must exude the characteristics of life. If the soul exists, it is devoid of all memories post mortem. If the soul exists, there is no reason it would maintain cohesion once released from its physical vessel, and like any other form of energy under the same circumstances, would dissipate.

So, maybe humans do have a soul, but if we apply elementary reasoning and common sense to the concept, there is nothing to suggest an afterlife. Perhaps, and unfortunately, life is more like a match: a spark of life from lifelessness, burns ever so briefly in the grand scheme of things, to which it finally withers and burns out, with only the residual smoke to dissipate and otherwise vanish.

Stigmata, Shroud and Fatima

Many Christians hold certain miracles sacred. While this is not an essay to challenge or question someone's particular faith, it is an essay to present elementary logic to three of the most commonly accepted miracles of Christianity. Again, this is not an attempt to invalidate the reader's belief system, but rather to invoke thought on each of these subjects and force the reader to review each with an objective eye.

The Miracle of Fatima allegedly occurred on October 13, 1917, which essentially makes it a modern miracle. To briefly paraphrase an eyewitness report, the following chronology of events occurred:

- *At approximately 1:30 pm, a column of thin, fine and bluish smoke extended up to perhaps two meters above the heads of the children, and evaporated at that height. This lasted less than a minute and repeated three times.*
- *The rain stopped and the overcast sky suddenly cleared.*

- *The sun shined seemingly brighter and stood out clearly in the sky, yet allowed onlookers to view it directly without hurting their eyes.*
- *The sun also appeared to have a "giddy" motion and "spun round upon itself."*
- *The atmosphere changed various colors, with an amethyst color being the most prominent.*
- *Suddenly, the sun, whirling wildly and blood red in color, seemed to fall from the heavens and advanced threateningly upon the earth, i.e. get much bigger in the sky as if it were crashing down from the sky.*
- *The sun receded and everything returned to normal.*[1]

So what does the Miracle of Fatima tell us? Actually, not much. But it does pose a whole lot of questions that need to be answered.

First, we know for a fact that the sun shines on half the Earth at any given time. If the sun really appeared to fall from the sky, why didn't anyone else in the world see it? The answer is obvious. The sun did not do anything at all. The events of the Miracle of Fatima are localized to Fatima. Therefore, whatever the people witnessed could very likely been the product of a localized atmospheric phenomenon.

Many strange and unusual phenomena occur in the atmosphere, the Aurora Borealis is probably the most common. This is not suggesting that the Aurora Borealis is the cause of

The Modern Paradigm of Liberty

the Miracle, but it does illustrate the unusual events that can occur naturally in the atmosphere beyond human control.

Second, what was the emission of smoke that immediately preceded the miracle? How and why would that relate to anything associated with the event? It serves no religious significance and is not directly linked to the miracle in the sky. So, what was it?

The answer is that it was very likely a natural emission of a gaseous substance. Further, many gases cause hallucinations when inhaled. This could have influenced the perception of the eyewitnesses. Further, the whole field may have been emitting the gases and only a high concentration was emitted near the children. The eyewitness report says that the smoke evaporated pretty quickly, suggesting that it would be invisible at low concentrations.

Third, why did the image appear to the children only and/or the miracle centered on the children? Further research on the miracle shows that only the eldest of the children claimed to actually see the image, while the other two children claimed to only hear the voice. In addition, they always encountered the vision at the same spot numerous times leading to the day of the miracle. Assuming the previous suggestion to be true, hallucinogenic gases concentrated around where the children were would likely account for their visions.

So, how could so many people witness the miracle? Simple, the human body has the same basic chemical make up from person to person. This would mean that a hallucinogenic agent would have the same affect on all them. Further, if an atmospheric disturbance were to occur, it would be clearly visible to all in attendance. Finally, all the witnesses were very devout Christians. They all made the pilgrimage to Fatima with the expectation of a miracle. Given the other mitigating factors suggested, a "miracle" in their eyes was more than likely a self-fulfilling prophecy.

The Shroud of Turin[2]: Although never official endorsed by the Catholic Church, the Shroud of Turin is recognized the world over by countless millions of Christians as the actual burial cloth of Jesus Christ. But is it really?

The story of the Shroud begins in April 1349 when a French Knight writes to Pope Clement VI that he intends to build a church in Lirey, France, and was already in possession of the Shroud at the time. The Shroud was believed to be acquired by the French Knight in Constantinople, but that was never confirmed.

Today, the debate still rages and, even though extensive examination and analysis by both religious leaders and scientists have been performed, the findings are still inconclusive. Some of the analysis suggest the age of the Shroud to be only 13th Century, making it only about 700 years old. This is consistent with the story of the French Knight.

If the Shroud were genuine, it should date to be approximately 2000 years. This suggests that the analysis proves that the Shroud is a forgery. But the initial analysis was later questioned as potentially flawed because the Shroud was exposed to a fire in 1532.

Since the historical accuracy cannot be accounted for, the validity of the artifact remains in question. So what should Christians do? Well, Thomas Jefferson once said that "Ignorance is preferable to error, and he is less remote from the truth who believes nothing than he who believes what is wrong." Following Jefferson's advice, the prudent approach should be to take the existing stance of neither confirming nor denying the validity of the Shroud. Instead, take the position that it is simply a historical curiosity like the Vineland Map, and nothing more.

But just for fun, let us assume as a fact that Jesus Christ is the Son of God and the Messiah as described in the Bible. Let us also assume that the Shroud is the actual Shroud of Jesus Christ. There are actual blood stains on the Shroud. Now, assuming cloning technology evolves sufficiently to the point where an extracted sample of DNA from the Shroud could be used, should we attempt to clone Jesus Christ? This would be a deliberately invoked second coming of Christ. This is a rhetorical question, presented merely as food for thought. You decide.

Stigmata*: bodily marks or pains resembling the wounds of the crucified Christ and sometimes accompanying religious ecstasy.*[3]

Many people throughout history have been sufferers of the wounds of Christ. They claim that their wounds are the product of divine intervention and, as a result, are a miracle. But are they? What are the consistencies and inconsistencies of the so-called stigmata miracle?

First, we can dismiss anyone whose wounds are self-inflicted. These examples of Stigmata are clearly not the product of any miracle. The only possibility remaining not attributed to divine intervention is psychosomatic.

What is very interesting about those who suffer stigmata are these important facts:

- *Over 80 percent of stigmata sufferers are women.*
- *They all have an unquestionable and deep devotion to Christianity.*
- *They all are highly susceptible to hypnosis.*
- *The consistencies of their wounds are only to that of their most frequently viewed image of the crucifixion, usually that represented in their parish.*[4]

These are all very interesting and suspicious correlations with all psychosomatic instances of stigmata. First, the fact that the overwhelming majority of stigmatists are women seems likely since women by nature are more emotionally empathic then men are. Add to this the second element of a deep seeded Christian devotion. People use their faiths as an emotional crutch and outlet. This creates a logical link between the two.

Third, being highly susceptible to hypnosis implies that stigmatists have both a weak mind as well as an open door to the subconscious. Further, hypnosis is often used to demonstrate human examples of mind over matter. Such examples include walking on hot coals and stiffening of the body like a board. Again, stigmata logically falls into this category of mind over matter as a rare example.

Finally, stigmatists do not suffer the actual wounds of Christ. During the period of the crucifixion, Romans crucified their prisoners by piercing their hands at the base, i.e. in the wrist. Even the Shroud of Turin represents these wounds of the hand to be in the wrists. However, most *genuine* stigmatists bleed from the center of their hand. So, either they are not suffering the wounds of Christ, or the Shroud of Turin is a forgery. A reasonable person cannot accept both.

Further, one of the wounds of Christ includes the injury Christ received in his side when pierced by a Roman spear. The Bible does not specify which side it was. So, some *genuine* stigmatists bleed on the right, while others bleed from the left. The only consistency being that the stigmatists suffer the wounds of Christ represented in their parish or most common representation of the crucifixion.

****

In short, most so-called miracles have logical and reasonable explanations associated with them. What is really occurring in the presence of miracles is an extraordinary event that some are attributing to divine intervention. But, extraordinary claims require extraordinary evidence. *Hume's rule in "Of Miracles" is that when an alleged miracle occurs we ask ourselves which would be more miraculous, the alleged miracle or that we are being hoaxed?*[5] A reasonable, rational and intelligent person should assume the latter first and then only the former in the presence of sufficient extraordinary evidence, if such evidence exists.

[1] *http://www.fatima.org/miracle.html*
[2] *http://www.shroud.com/ (all information about the Shroud of Turin used in this essay was found on this web site)*
[3] *http://www.m-w.com/cgi-bin/dictionary, search word "Stigmata".*
[4] Arthur C. Clarke World of Strange Powers: *"Stigmata-The Wounds of Christ"*
[5] *http://skepdic.com/stigmata.html*

Fatima Correction: Because of conflicting reports about whether all three children or only the eldest child witnessed the vision of the Virgin Mary, this statement is retracted.

In God We Trust

For well over a century, the fraise "In God We Trust" has appeared in many places controlled or sponsored by various levels of government. The most common occurrence to the average American is that on our currency. This phrase has appeared on just about every piece of U.S. currency, coin and paper, throughout the twentieth century and exists today. The question is, should it appear at all? In this author's opinion, the answer is a definitive **No**.

The knee-jerk position of opposition is that of the separation of church and state. While the separation of church and state position is generically explored in another discussion, this particular instance in simply another example where religious beliefs are propagated by government. But that aside, is "In God We Trust" on U.S. currency in conflict with those who find Judeo-Christian doctrine sacred?

In the original version of the Ten Commandments, the third commandment is "Thou shalt not make unto me any ungraven image." In other words, man if forbidden by God make any image of God and recognize/worship that image as God.

This is often used as a reference to forbid idol worship. But this also refers to writing the name of God and treating it with any sanctity. Those who support the word "God" on U.S. currency are treating it with that same sense of sanctity. In short, the presence of the word "God" on U.S. currency overtly violates one of the basic tenets of the original Ten Commandments.

Furthermore, for any Christian or Jew to defend "God" on U.S. currency would be to lend religious value to the word "God" as they would be worshiping and valuing an image of God as if it were as important as God itself. Thus they would be personally violating the Ten Commandments themselves. How could any good Christian or Jew support "God" on U.S. currency and not be in conflict with core doctrine of their faith?

Further, currency is associated with many of the great sins and crimes of our society. These include greed, theft, bribery, embezzlement, drug dealing, prostitution, etc. Money has even been called the **root of all evil**. Isn't that like putting "God" on a pentagram? Even further, money is the epitome of materialism and the furthest thing from being spiritual. Finally, all paper money is ultimately destroyed, so the U.S.

Government regularly destroys images of the Judeo-Christian God. See the point?

Think about how abused money is. Look through your wallet right now and you will probably find a worn and beaten bill. Think about where that bill has been, whose hands they changed, and what it was used for. Think of all the ails of society and which ones this particular bill is associated with. Finally, put the bill back in your wallet and, like many people, put your wallet in your back pocket. Is it respectful for you to take a stack of paper with God's name all over it and rub it up against your ass all day long, not to mention sit on it?

A 1972 research study that appeared in the Journal of the American Medical Association (one of the first of its kind) has even shown that both paper and coin currency have traces of Staphylococcus aureus bacteria (about 10 percent) and fecal coliform bacteria (about 40 percent), which indicates contact with human feces.[1]

Further studies performed by the FBI on samples from New York, Miami, Houston, and San Francisco, have found traces of cocaine on 90 percent of paper money, particularly on bills in denominations of $20 or higher that are older, warn and well-circulated.[1]

What disturbs me is that the separation of church and state argument is the only argument posed in this debate. When, in reality, those people of truly devout faith should be outraged that the sacred name of God appears on something so disrespectful. In fact, it is outright public blasphemy sponsored by the United States government and paid for by the American taxpayer.

[1] *http://www.s-t.com/daily/03-01/03-22-01/a02wn009.htm*

The Separation of Church and State

Ever since Thomas Jefferson coined the term "separation of church and state" in a letter to the Baptists of Danbury, Connecticut, the debate of what this concept really means has been in dispute. The obvious fact is, in a truly free society, government should remain neutral on all fronts and defend the rights of individuals from the tyranny of the majority.

The problem with a purely democratic society that is *not* a republic is that it allows for an infringement of individual rights, which is why the founders established this nation as a republic and asserted such individual liberties within the Bill of Rights. But this alone does not solve the issue and/or satisfy the opinions of those who believe that religious influence on government is acceptable.

Jefferson's words in the above mentioned letter is the only specific enumeration of the "separation of church and state" from the period of the founders that this author is aware of.

This term does **not** specifically appear in any founding document, most notably the U.S. Constitution. The obvious question is; should it appear at all? Not necessarily.

As discussed earlier, the mission of the U.S. Constitution is three-fold; define the structure of government, define the power of government, and enumerate the rights of the people. This mission is clear to the casual observer based on the language in the U.S. Constitution. So, given the mission, would we expect to see the phrase "separation of church and state" in the U.S. Constitution, even if that were specifically the founders' intent? Probably not.

The reason why the phrase "separation of church and state" would logically not appear in the U.S. Constitution is because it would not be consistent with one of its three missions. More specifically, the concept of "separation of church and state" is a **restriction** on both government and the people, and the U.S. Constitution is not a list of government or citizen restrictions (see early discussion describing the Mission of the U.S. Constitution).

While those people who contend that the U.S. Constitution does not specifically state "separation of church and state", the U.S. Constitution also does **not** state, imply or support "God", "Jesus", "Ten Commandments", "Christianity", or "Christ" either. Does the absence of pro-religious references imply that government should be Atheist? Absolutely not. It just means that government should be religiously neutral.

The movement by those opposed to the separation of church and state continue to present so-called *evidence* that this is a *godly* nation with specific *Judeo-Christian* roots, using the personal beliefs and actions of the founders. While the **personal** religious practices of many of the founders included deism, even devout Christianity, their **formal** position on the linkage between religion and government is conspicuous by the blatant absence of pro-religious references in the U.S. Constitution.

If the founders **really** wanted to ensure God and/or Judeo-Christian beliefs in formal society and/or in government, they could have done so with a single sentence in the U.S. Constitution. They didn't. Instead, they did the opposite and intentionally omitted all references that would support any generic or specific religious principle.

What the founders did do was make two very specific references for religious freedom and protection from prejudice and persecution. The first and most commonly recognized language is in the First Amendment, which states that "Congress shall make no law respecting an establishment of religion, or prohibiting the free exercise thereof."

However, the second reference in the U.S. Constitution is more important language that asserts that the U.S. government should remain religiously neutral. This text appears in the last paragraph of Article VI. It states that while all federal and state legislators, executives and judicial officers are bound by oath or affirmation to support the constitution, ***"no religious test shall ever be required as a qualification to any office or public trust under the United States."*** This protection allows for someone overtly anti-Christian to be elected or appointed to any public office, even President.

So, if the founders really wanted the United States to truly be godly and/or Judeo-Christian, why would they intentionally go out of their way to include such language which specifically prevents government from disqualifying people from serving in government based on their religious beliefs? Keep in mind that Article VI was written and ratified two years **before** the Bill of Rights.

While this enumerates that government cannot assert religious authority, does the U.S. Constitution imply a restriction on the people to use religion to influence government? **Yes**. Again, the mission of U.S. Constitution includes enumerating the rights of the people. The limitations of a citizen's rights in a free society exist when the actions of one person or group infringe on the rights of another person or group.

Since government is, by design, governing *all* the people, and since religious beliefs are subjective to only *some* of the people, then religious influence on government implies that some people exercising their freedom of religion would be forcibly imposing their subjective religious belief on others by way of government endorsement and action. This overtly infringes on some people's free exercise of their religion as it forces them to subscribe to a religious principle endorsed and sponsored by the secular authority, particularly if that religious principle is contrary to their own.

Despite the above, is the United States really built on Judeo-Christian/godly principles? **Yes** and **No**. Arguably, many of the principles and laws of the nation's founding can be traced to Judeo-Christian references. But, are those the **roots** of these principles?

The basic concepts of a Democracy and a Republic overtly predate the existence of Christianity with prima facie evidence rooting these concepts in societies that celebrated the polytheistic faiths of Greco-Roman origin, faiths that contemporary Judeo-Christian belief systems would otherwise construe as pagan.

This discussion is not an attempt to alter the reader's perception of the **personal** religious practices of the founders. Instead, it should invoke objective thought about the issue of the separation of church and state. Ironically, the more religious the founding fathers are perceived to be, the more it suggests that the founders wanted to keep religion out of government by the verbatim secular language in the U.S. Constitution. This is evident due to intentional omission of pro-religious references as the U.S. Constitution exists as an overtly secular and religiously neutral document.

And what is the harm if our government is religiously neutral? There is no harm, especially *if* you truly celebrate a society where everyone can experience freedom to the fullest potential, as long as they *respect* the freedoms of others.

But maybe there is some harm to governmental religious neutrality. That harm would be on those manipulating the religious majority. The harm is, they would lose real power over all people and government would no longer be a sponsor for their subjective messages.

Besides, the founders wanted the citizens to aspire towards freedom, particularly religious freedom. Many of the early settlers fled other areas of the world to come to the *new world* because of religious persecution. The founders wanted to be sure that no citizen would ever feel the need to flee the United States for the same reason. Rather, the United States would be the beacon of hope for anyone who wishes to express any religious beliefs freely. But that's a little hard to do when government sponsors and validates some religious beliefs (ex. monotheism), which by design undermines and invalidates other religious beliefs (ex. polytheism, non-theism, etc.).

Summary

So, there you have it, one man's perspective on contemporary American issues. It was my intention to share with the reader these thoughts in the hopes that you recognize you don't have to subscribe to the opinions of a handful of political mouth pieces with narrow subjective agendas promoted by the self-serving media outlets. What you should take away with from this book is not only a unique analysis on these subjects, but the empowerment to form your own opinions based on your own subjective perspectives, information, research and viewpoint.

In a free society, we enjoy the freedom of speech. Unfortunately, most free speech is exercised by a small minority of people who are self-proclaimed subject matter experts. But the only subject matter expert on your opinions is you. Take the power this book has provided you with and force yourself to create your own positions on these and other issues.

Don't let others decide your opinions and beliefs for you, especially if their positions are rooted in narrow-minded rhetoric centuries old or are those willing to compromise individual liberties for the greater good. You have the power to shape your own future, and the future of this great nation. Seize it.

Favorite Quotes of the Author

"If ye love wealth better than liberty, the tranquility of servitude better than the animated contest of freedom, go home from us in peace. We ask not your counsel or arms. Crouch down and lick the hands which feed you. May your chains set lightly upon you, and may posterity forget that ye were our countrymen."
- Samuel Adams

*****

"Freedom is never more than one generation away from extinction."
- Ronald Reagan

*****

"Free speech does not protect the speech that you like, it protects the speech that you hate."
- Larry Flynt

*****

"Patriots are not revolutionaries trying to overthrow government. Patriots are counter-revolutionaries trying to prevent government from overthrowing the U.S. Constitution."
- Author unknown

*****

"The care of human life and happiness, and not their destruction, is the first and only legitimate object of good government."
- Thomas Jefferson, to the Republican Citizens of Washington County, Maryland, March 31, 1809

*****

"Free men are not equal. Equal men are not free."
- Author unknown

*****

"When you have eliminated the impossible, that which remains, however improbable, must be the truth."
- Sir Arthur Conan Doyle

*****

"In the beginning of change, the patriot is a scarce man; brave, hated and scorned. When his cause succeeds however, the timid join him, for then it costs nothing to be a patriot."
- Mark Twain

*****

"To compel a man to furnish funds for the propagation of ideas he disbelieves and abhors is sinful and tyrannical."
- Thomas Jefferson

*****

"Sometimes the majority means that all the fools are on the same side"
- Author unknown

*****

A Democracy: Three wolves and a sheep voting on dinner.

A Republic: The flock gets to vote for which wolves vote on dinner.

A Constitutional Republic: Voting on dinner is expressly forbidden, and the sheep are armed.

Federal Government: The means by which the sheep will be fooled into voting for a Democracy.
- Author unknown

*****

"Liberty is the difference between the free thought of individuals and the actions of free individuals."
- Author unknown

*****

"Creativity is a gift of nature, the only true measurement of which is the difference between its product and the sum of its raw material."
- Sean McPhillips

*****

"Cream always rises to the top. But then again, so do impurities."
- Sean McPhillips

*****

"I may not agree with what you have to say, but I will fight to the death for your right to say it."
- Patrick Henry

*****

"An armed citizenry insures liberty."
- Sean McPhillips

*****

Tolerance: When the Majority willfully accepts the beliefs and practices of the Minority.

Dominance: When the Minority is forcibly subjected to the beliefs and practices of the Majority.
- Sean McPhillips

*****

"If cowardly and dishonorable men sometimes shoot unarmed men with army pistols or guns, the evil must be met by the penitentiary and gallows, and not by a general deprivation of a constitutional privilege."
- Arkansas State Supreme Court, 1878

*****

"A lie told often enough becomes the truth."
- Lenin (1870 - 1924)

*****

If the Arabs put down their weapons today, there would be no more Violence.
If the Jews put down their weapons today, there would be no more Israel.
- Author unknown

*****

"After a shooting spree, they always want to take the guns away from the people who didn't do it."
- William S. Burroughs

*****

"Those who would trade liberty for security deserves neither liberty nor security."
- Benjamin Franklin

*****

"Ignorance is preferable to error, and he is less remote from the truth who believes nothing than he who believes what is wrong."
-Thomas Jefferson (Notes on Virginia, 1782)

*****

"Millions of innocent men, women and children, since the introduction of Christianity, have been burnt, tortured, fined and imprisoned; yet we have not advanced one inch towards uniformity."
-Thomas Jefferson, Notes on Virginia, 1782

*****

"But it does me no injury for my neighbor to say there are twenty gods or no God. It neither picks my pocket nor breaks my leg."
-Thomas Jefferson, Notes on Virginia, 1782.

*****

"Question with boldness even the existence of a god; because if there be one he must approve of the homage of reason more than that of blindfolded fear."
-Thomas Jefferson, Letter to Peter Carr, August 10, 1787

*****

"In every country and in every age, the priest has been hostile to liberty. He is always in alliance with the despot, abetting his abuses in return for protection to his own."
-Thomas Jefferson, letter to Horatio G. Spafford, March 17, 1814